Quilting has truly become an international endeavor. A [...] to explore beyond the boundaries of the country you live in to experience and see what other fiber artists are doing.

In many countries, rather than learning from various books, quilters study under a single master, spending years progressing from simple techniques to the extremely difficult. This is particularly true in Japan. Intricate designs are celebrated, and sewing and quilting by hand is honored. As such, hand quilting is the typical method used to quilt.

This book was written in its original language, Japanese, by a master quilter, Yoko Saito. We have done our best to make the directions for each project easy to understand if you have some level of quilting experience, while maintaining the book's appearance and the intent of the author and original publisher.

In Japan, houses tend to be small without much wall space for large hangings. Traditionally, Japanese have used futons for sleeping rather than western-style beds, so bed quilts are also not as common; thus you will often see small projects and bags rather than larger bed-sized quilts.

We hope the beautifully designed handmade items in this book inspire and encourage you to make them for yourself.

- Important Tips Before You Begin -

The following facts might suggest that intermediate or advanced quilters will be more comfortable working on these projects.

- Techniques -

Beyond the step-by-step lessons (in pictures on pp. 56–63), Ms. Saito does not go into detailed descriptions of specific quilting or sewing methods for each project. She assumes that the creator is familiar with sewing, quilting, and bag-making techniques to some degree and thus relies heavily on the creator's ability to figure out the directions that are not specifically written out. It is advisable to read through and understand each project's direction page from beginning to end, including finding the corresponding patterns on the included pattern sheets, before beginning.

- Measurements -

The original designs were created using the metric system for dimensions. In order to assist you, we have included the imperial system measurements in brackets. However, please note that samples that appear in the book were created and tested using the metric system. Thus, you will find that if you use the imperial measurements to make the projects, the items you make will not be exactly the same size as when using the metric measurements.

- Patterns/Templates -

Full pattern information for each project appears in several different ways: a) in the materials list, b) in the illustrations and captions, and c) in the pattern sheet insert. One must read through all the instructions carefully to understand what size to cut the fabric and related materials, including instructions for each project relating to seam allowances.

- Notions/Accessories -

Some of the projects in this book call for a variety of accessories such as zippers, handles, and hardware. While the originals were made with items from Japan, most if not all of the accessories shown have comparable items or are available around the world. Some of the accessories, however, are available through Yoko Saito's quilt shop in Japan. See the copyright page for further information.

Stitch Publications, 2019

Yoko Saito's

I Love Houses

Introduction

If I were asked what motif I would never tire of making in my life, I would have to say house blocks and appliqués. I think that many who do patchwork and quilting love houses as well. Designing these houses out of fabric is almost like building a real house.

In my first book on this subject, *Houses, Houses, Houses,* which was published more than 10 years ago, most of the houses were modeled after houses that I consider American in style. Perhaps this is because I was first introduced to quilts in America, and that is where I had spent the most time traveling. However, in the last decade I have had the opportunity to go to mainland Europe and the Scandinavian countries quite often. I began to notice the different styles of the houses in this different climate and culture and how they were designed and built.

As I visited various cities, towns, and villages, I rarely saw two houses with the same design. In fact, the shapes, colors, number of doors and windows, as well as roof lines were often completely different. Perhaps this is a reflection of a culture that honors the tradition of handicrafts.

In this book I have tried to introduce some projects that are not as difficult to make, in hopes that you will enjoy the process of creating them. To this end, for some of the projects I have chosen to use single pieces of cloth instead of more complicated piecing for the backgrounds. You will see some bird motifs, but my imagination also runs wild with the people living in these houses. They share their houses with animals and find inspiration in the surrounding environments. Maybe this is why I so love houses—they reflect the warmth of the world around us.

Yoko Saito

Contents

Project Title	Pages	Pattern Sheet
Simple Silhouette Bag	6 • 64	D
Village Tote	8 • 66	A
City Skyline Wall Hanging	10 • 68	A
Pencil Case	12 • 69	C
Spring • Summer • Autumn • Winter	14 • 70	A
Winter Birds Clasp Purse	16 • 76	D
Boston Bag	18 • 72	C
Bread Basket	22 • 74	C
Lunch Bag	24 • 77	D
Shoulder Bag	26 • 78	B
Bottle Carrier	28 • 80	A
Zippered Sewing Case	30 • 81	B
House Pouch	32 • 56	C
Market Bag	34 • 84	D
Everyday Handbag	38 • 85	B
Pass Cases	40 • 88	C
Sewing Box	42 • 90	C
Flat Pouch	44 • 71	C
Glasses Case	46 • 93	D
Alsace Lorraine Wall Hanging	48 • 95	B
Quilting Basics	50	
Essential Quilting Notions & Tools	51	
Quilting Notions & Accessories Needed for Projects	52	
Hand Stitches & Embroidery Stitches	53	
Secrets to Choosing the Right Fabrics	54	

A

B

Simple Silhouette Bag

Appliquéd silhouettes of houses add a clever twist to a simple bag. Choose two neutral pieces of fabric for each side of the bag. Add the appliqué and embroidery to one side. It is an easy bag for any beginner to try.

→ page 64

C

Village Tote

There is no need to worry about symmetry or perfect shapes when you make this bag. The houses are so much more fun when you get creative. Orange siding, a yellow door, multiple windows . . . anything goes. Use dark-colored fabric for the background pieces to ground the overall effect.

→ page 66

City Skyline Wall Hanging

I like to hang quilts in the hallway of my home so that I can see them often. I've combined building styles from all over the world to create a city skyline. Birds fly above the buildings, and when I look at this quilt, I can almost hear the sounds of a city.

→ page 68

Pencil Case

The embroidered windows and doors of the buildings look like little faces. Use different colored fabrics for the various buildings to make them stand out from the background and each other. I used different yarn-dyed wovens or wools that look good together for the different sections of the pencil case body as well as the gusset.

→ page 69

Spring • Summer • Autumn • Winter

Each of the buildings for these seasons are similar to those that I have seen on my travels to Sweden. I love to imagine the families that live their lives in these wonderful little houses. Using fabric to depict the sky during different seasons is something I often like to do. → page 70

Winter Birds Clasp Purse

A building and bare trees blend into the frosty landscape. Little pops of color—an orange bird, a blue roof—stand out against the winter sky that, in Sweden, looks like grayish milk.

→ page 76

Boston Bag

The three-dimensional houses on the front side of the bag trick the eye with this design that was inspired by a Pandora's Box patchwork pattern. The back side is one piece of machine-quilted fabric and a large pocket.

→ page 72

Bread Basket

The winter nights can be long and dark in Northern Europe. The warm light shining through the windows warms my heart just as surely as it must warm the family tucked inside. The sides and bottom of this basket are constructed using sturdy template plastic. You might also use it as a napkin holder or to store accessories.
→ page 74

Lunch Bag

A house with a brightly striped roof is a fun design for the side of this lunch bag, which is large enough to hold many different kinds of containers. It is made of four pieces; two become the handle, while the opposite two can be tied together to keep things secure.

→ page 77

Shoulder Bag

I like to make bags that are comfortable and usable for when I travel. I put in zippers for the main bag opening as well as on the side for extra security. The shoulder strap has hardware to shorten or lengthen for a customized fit, so that it can be worn as a cross-body bag as well. I love the little visual surprises, like the small house that I appliquéd onto the bag body.

→ page 78

Bottle Carrier

I have found that bags in a cylindrical shape are unexpectedly more useful than I supposed. I use them to carry bottled water or a folding umbrella. This bag was made to look like a part of a castle or turret. The yarn-dyed woven fabric reminds me of stone or masonry.

→ page 80

Zippered Sewing Case

I always carry some sort of sewing pouch or case with me when I travel, and one with a zipper to keep everything secure is a must. This size is perfect because it holds quite a lot and even has a zippered pouch on the inside of the lid. The houses on the front with the appliquéd and embroidered tree make me think of a warm spring day. I often design my quilting to look like the wind blowing, as I've done on this project.

→ page 81

House Pouch

Can one ever have enough pouches for all the little things and accessories we collect?
When I look at this small pouch I think to myself that if I had a friend who lived in such
a cute house, I would want to drop by almost every day. Use your imagination and
creativity to add embroidery and embellishments.

→ page 56

Market Bag

Adding appliquéd and embroidered designs to a simple market bag makes you want to carry it all the more. These little ladybugs live in a mushroom house but eat at their picnic table outside when the weather is nice. You can easily enlarge the pattern pieces to customize the bag and create a size that works for you.

→ page 84

Everyday Handbag

I designed a handbag replica of a building that houses a restaurant. Similar buildings can be found all over Europe. I think of all the delicious food and happy diners inside when I look at it. It is roomy enough to carry quite a bit, with two outside pockets for those things you need to reach easily. The zippered bag opening folds up to become the roof when you are carrying it.

→ page 85

B   A

Pass Cases

I always have a pass case attached to my bags or purses for when I ride the train or bus. These are much cuter than ones I can find in the store. Your passes or cards can slide in on the back side right at the roof line, and the strap can be adjusted to any length. If you want to use these as luggage tags, replace the fabric on the back with clear vinyl.

→ page 88

Sewing Box

This is a great sewing box to keep around your house or sewing studio. It is a sturdy little box that holds quite a few things and has interior pockets for scissors or other slim notions. Putting a pincushion on the underside of the roof was the perfect solution to help the roof keep its shape. Don't you love it?

→ page 90

Flat Pouch

It can be inconvenient when small items get lost in your purse or bag. A mini pouch, such as this one in the shape of a house, is perfect for stashing those things. Using a brightly colored zipper is a fun thing to do.

→ page 71

Glasses Case

I wear glasses and prefer to have cute cases to store them in, both for home and on the go. I lined the case with a soft flannel so as not to damage the lenses.
I also used a machine stitch in the center of the gusset to make it easier to fold.
A magnet hidden inside the tabs keeps the case closed when necessary.

→ page 93

Alsace Lorraine Wall Hanging

I absolutely love the Alsace Lorraine territory of France with its hints of German design. The colors of the roofs and styles of buildings are amazing and beautiful. This small wall hanging is what I see in my mind's eye when I think of this region. All of the houses and buildings are a bit different, but they work wonderfully together with the landscape in the background.

→ page 95

Quilting Basics

All measurements listed for the following projects are in centimeters (cm) and in inches [in brackets].

• The dimensions of the finished projects are shown in the drawings.

• Note that the quilted pieces tend to shrink somewhat, depending on the type of fabric used, the thickness of the batting, the amount of quilting, and individual quilting technique. Double-check your quilted pieces against the pattern dimensions.

• The type of thread you should use for various techniques is not necessarily specified in the instructions. Use sewing thread for piecing by hand or machine, quilting thread for quilting, and embroidery floss for embroidery stitches.

• Choose a quilting-thread color that matches the fabric that you are quilting. Alternatively, you can use a beige or taupe color for the entire project.

• Seam allowances must be added; see each pattern for specific information for each piece. Add 0.3 to 0.5 cm [⅛" to scant ¼"] for appliqué, 0.7 cm [¼"] for piecing.

• For portions of the handbags, as well as the quilting, a sewing machine may be used. However, all the projects can be made by hand. If you do choose to sew by hand, use a backstitch.

Essential Quilting Notions & Tools

1. Nonslip Board: The nonslip surface board is used when marking fabric or when using the fabric pressing tool to turn under the seam allowances. The soft side, backed with batting and fabric, can be used as a mini ironing surface.

2. Quilting Hoop: Used to hold the quilt sandwich during quilting.

3. Embroidery Hoop: Used to hold fabric taut while doing embroidery.

4. Weights (paperweight, beanbag, etc.): Used to weigh down a small quilt when quilting.

5. Iron: A small portable iron is used to press pieced seams.

6. Rulers: Used to trace straight lines when transferring patterns. Rulers with markings made for quilters are useful.

7. Scissors: They will last longer if each pair is used for specific things, such as for paper, fabric, or thread.

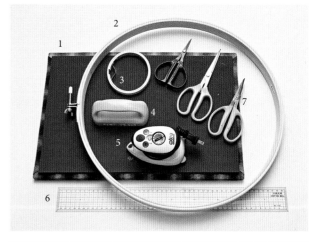

8. Light Table: Used to transfer pattern from a pattern sheet to fabric to mark the location and/or design for appliqué and embroidery.

9. Thimbles: Used to protect your fingers while quilting.

   a. Ceramic Thimble: Used to push needle through cloth when quilting.

   b. Metal Thimble: Used to push needle through cloth when quilting.

   c. Leather Thimble: Slip this under the porcelain or metal thimble as you work to keep the outer thimble from slipping.

10. Leather Ring: Used on the middle finger of right hand while doing piecework to push needle and thread through the fabric while you sew.

11. Rubber Finger Tip: Wear on your right index finger during quilting or appliqué to help grab the needle and reduce slippage.

12. Thread Cutter Ring: Conveniently worn on your left (or right) thumb and used for cutting threads as you are working. Refer to p. 60 for how to use items 9–12.

13. Pencils • Chalk Pencils: Used for copying patterns or marking quilting lines. If you use a pencil to mark quilting lines, use one with soft lead. The lines won't always disappear, so be careful if using a pencil to mark quilting lines.

14. Seam Pressing Tools (Hera markers): Used to press seam allowances down in lieu of ironing when working with appliqué pieces.

   a. Seam Presser Hera

   b. Appliqué Hera

15. Awl: To mark points when transferring and drawing patterns. Also useful for turning under seam allowances.

16. Spoon: Often used when pin basting a quilt. Safety pins are easy to use for this method.

17. Push pins: Useful to keep layers from shifting when getting ready to baste the quilt sandwich. The longer the pin, the better.

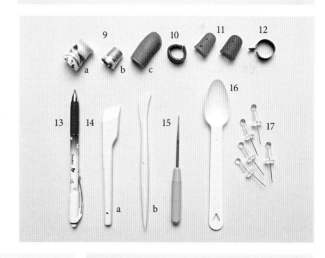

18. Needles:

   a. Basting Needles: Long needles used for basting.

   b/c. Patchwork/Piecing Needles: Sharp, thin pins that slide easily through fabric layers (use stronger needles for heavier fabric).

   d. Quilting Betweens: Shorter than Sharps; used for quilting.

   e. Embroidery Needles: With larger eyes for easy threading, they are also pointed for smooth piercing (not pictured).

19. Pins:

   a. Appliqué: Small heads that can be easily passed over by the surface of an iron; the short length keeps them from catching loose threads.

   b. Piecing: Slightly longer and useful for piecing fabrics together.

20. Thread:

   a. Basting Thread: Used for basting.

   b/c. Sewing Thread: Used for piecing or stitching; appropriate for either hand sewing or machine sewing; polyester or cotton (50 wt).

   d. Quilting Thread: A coated, durable thread that is slightly thicker than most thread and is used for hand quilting.

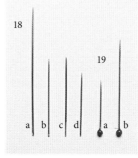

Quilting Notions & Accessories Needed for Projects

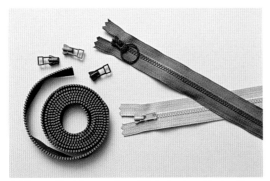

A. Zippers: Used for security and fastening two sides together. [Boston Bag (p. 18); House Pouch (p. 32); Everyday Handbag (p. 38); etc.]

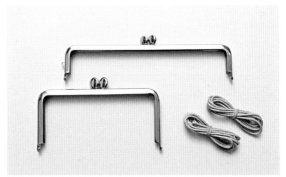

B. Metal Purse Frame: Used as a closure for smaller bags, pouches or purses. [Pencil Case (p. 12); Winter Birds Clasp Purse (p. 16)]

C. Tulle (netting): Used for an inside pocket to allow someone to easily see what is inside. [Zippered Sewing Case (p. 30)]

D. Woven Webbing (linen, cotton, or nylon): Used for straps and handles. [Boston Bag (p. 18); Shoulder Bag (p. 26); etc.]

E. Straps and Cords (leather or woven): Used as a lanyard on smaller objects, pouches, or purses.

F. Picture Frames: Used to frame mini quilted projects.

G. Template Material (plastic or board): Durable and sturdy; used for bottoms and sides of quilted projects. [Bread Basket (p. 22); Sewing Box (p. 42)]

H. Key Chain Hardware: Used to connect cords and straps to small quilted pouches or purses.

Hand Stitches

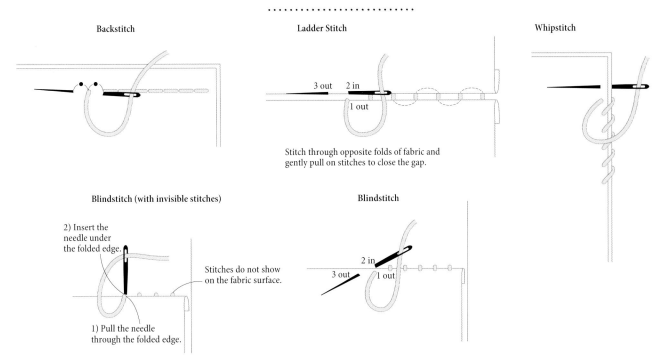

Backstitch

Ladder Stitch

Whipstitch

Stitch through opposite folds of fabric and gently pull on stitches to close the gap.

Blindstitch (with invisible stitches)

2) Insert the needle under the folded edge.

Stitches do not show on the fabric surface.

1) Pull the needle through the folded edge.

Blindstitch

2 in

3 out

1 out

Embroidery Stitches

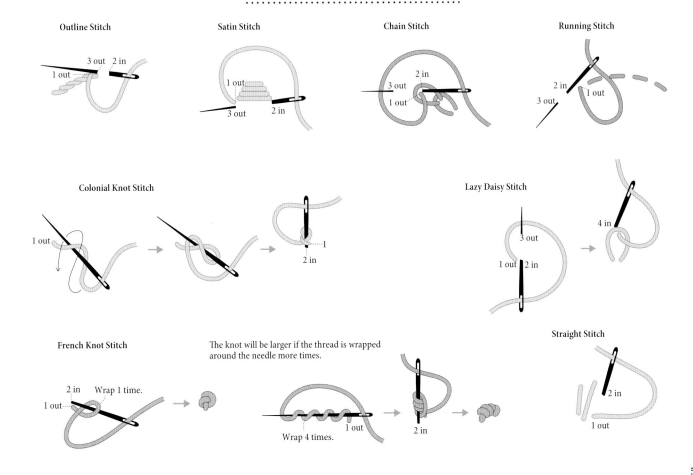

Outline Stitch

3 out 2 in
1 out

Satin Stitch

1 out
3 out 2 in

Chain Stitch

2 in
3 out
1 out

Running Stitch

2 in
3 out 1 out

Colonial Knot Stitch

1 out

1
2 in

Lazy Daisy Stitch

3 out
1 out 2 in

4 in

French Knot Stitch

2 in Wrap 1 time.
1 out

The knot will be larger if the thread is wrapped around the needle more times.

Wrap 4 times. 1 out

2 in

Straight Stitch

2 in
1 out

Secrets to Choosing the Right Fabrics

I have loved gazing at fabric since I was a little girl. I have been designing fabric for about 20 years now. Many of my ideas for projects and new ways of using fabric came out of the fabric-designing process. I would like to use the projects in this book to introduce some key points in making your finished projects look even better.

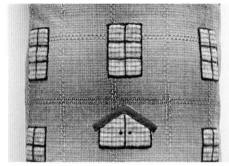

Bottle Carrier → p. 28

Bread Basket → p. 22

Market Bag → p. 34

Spring • Summer • Autumn • Winter → p. 14

Spring • Summer • Autumn • Winter → p. 14

Using fabric to create different effects

Take a closer look at the fabric and imagine how to arrange it to bring out its patterns, contrast in colors, and texture. For example, fabric with gradated colors can depict unevenness or aging of walls (see Bottle Carrier). You can also use places where the fabric color changes in gradated fabric to create dividers in your block. Checked fabrics can be used to depict windows with mullions (see Bread Basket).

Fabrics with specific motifs printed on them, such as wood, leaves, and flowers, can work as a background on their own. Taking things further, polka dots can be used for a mushroom cap (see Market Bag), leaf prints can be used for woods, or a scuffed-up white pattern on black can mimic the Milky Way (see Spring • Summer • Autumn • Winter) to create a wider variety of effects.

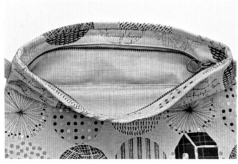

Shoulder Bag → p. 26

Village Tote → p. 8

Winter Birds Clasp Purse → p. 16

Choosing practical and fashionable lining

For bags and pouches, I usually use a brighter lining to make the inside more visible. I recommend avoiding white or light solid-color fabric (which shows stains easily) and choosing prints in bright colors with subtle contrast. You can create a sense of unity by choosing the lining in the same color tone as the outside (see Shoulder Bag), or if the outside is in a light color or dark color, you can be playful by choosing a check for the lining (see Village Tote or Winter Birds Clasp Purse). Seeing your favorite pattern every time you open your bag or pouch will brighten your mood.

Zippered Sewing Case ➞ p. 30

Sewing Box ➞ p. 42

Boston Bag ➞ p. 18

Textures created with quilting

The effects of quilting are not limited to mimicking scenery. Quilting can also accent blocks to make appliqués look more realistic or to depict softness, sharpness, or other textures. Spending time and effort on quilting will add rich expression to your projects. I quilt the background fabric so that the fabric print and quilting lines are in harmony (see Zippered Sewing Case). In some projects I quilt a little irregularly to create an idyllic atmosphere (see Sewing Box). In other projects, to add a touch of masculinity, I quilt very simple lines (Boston Bag).

Pass Case B ➞ p. 40

Pass Case A ➞ p. 40

Flat Pouch ➞ p. 44

Using highlight color

Recently, I have started using red, yellow, blue, and other brighter colors in many of my projects. It may be difficult to use these colors as backgrounds, but they can be added as highlights if used as small door or window pieces. Or you can add a brighter color to a checked background as an accent.

Brushed flannels give softer impressions of their colors and prints and are useful in creating just the right amount of brightness. I have also used the wrong side of fabric for less vivid patterns or irregularity of patterns (see Pass Cases and Flat Pouch).

I recommend accumulating experience in looking at a variety of fabrics to cultivate a discerning eye for it. It is also important to research beautiful color combinations and materials from scenery on your vacations, paintings, or photographs in addition to actual patchwork projects that you like. But the most important thing of all is not to be afraid of making mistakes. I have made countless mistakes up to now. Even now, I continue to tell myself, "I should have done it this way" every day. Try out new things such as using the wrong side of fabric, experimenting with unusual pattern combinations, or using non-quilting fabric. If you keep trying different things, you'll come across surprisingly good affinities.

House Pouch shown on p. 32

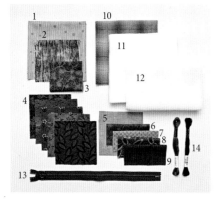

Finished Measurements

Length (l): 11 cm [4⅜"]; width (w): 18 cm [7⅛"];
bag bottom gusset width (w): 4 cm [1½"]

The full-size design is on side C of the pattern
sheet inserts.

To make these instructions easy to understand,
some of the thread colors used in the pictures
that follow are different from those specified
in the "Materials Needed" section.

Materials Needed

Cottons:
1 Light gray print - 30 x 25 cm [12" x 10"] (front
and back pouch background, lower gusset sides)
2 Brown print - 15 x 20 cm [6" x 8"] (pouch
bottom, pieces E and G)
3 Dark gray print - 15 x 30 cm [6" x 12"] (upper
gusset)
4 5 blue-gray prints - 10 x 12 cm [4" x 5"] each
(roof pieces)
5 Sand print - 10 x 10 cm [4" x 4"] (piece D)
6 Green print - 6 x 6 cm [3" x 3"] (piece F)
7 Dark brown check - 5 x 10 cm [2" x 4"]
(piece C)
8 Dark brown print - 12 x 11 cm [5" x 4½"]
(piece B, tab)
9 Red print - 10 x 10 cm [4" x 4"] (piece A)
10 Light check - 100 x 50 cm [40" x 20"]
(backing, bias binding for seam allowances)
Other supplies:
11 Batting - 50 x 30 cm [20" x 12"]
12 Double-sided fusible batting - 40 x 45 cm
[16" x 18"]
13 Zipper - 25 cm [10"] or longer
14 Embroidery floss: black and gray
You will also need interfacing (35 x 10 cm)
[14" x 4"] (not shown).

Dimensional Diagram

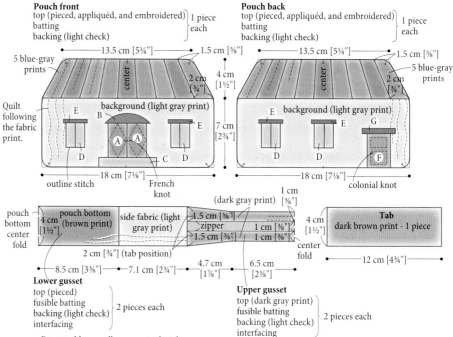

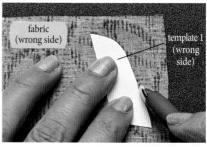

- Do not add seam allowances to the tab.
- When cutting roof pieces for the pouch front and back, add 0.7 cm [¼"] seam allowances. For appliqués, add 0.3 to 0.4 cm [⅛"] seam allowances; except add 1 cm [⅜"] seam allowances for the bottom edge of pieces C and F. Add 3 cm [1¼"] seam allowances to backing and batting. Cut out background pieces for pouch front and back with 1 cm [⅜"] seam allowances.
- For the lower gusset, do not add seam allowance to the interfacing. For the backing, add 3 cm [1¼"] seam allowance. For all other lower gusset pieces, add 1 cm [⅜"] seam allowances.
- For the upper gusset, do not add seam allowance to the interfacing; cut the other pieces with 2 cm [¾"] seam allowances except for the edges where the zipper is installed (for that, add 1 cm [⅜"] seam allowances).
- Cut 2 pieces each of bias binding for seam allowances from light check (2.5 x 10 cm [1" x 4"] and 2.5 x 63 cm [1" x 24¾"]).

1. Cutting out pouch pieces

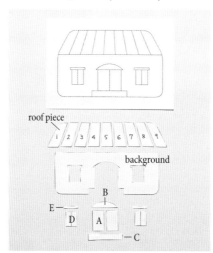

1 Prepare two pieces of the front pouch template. Cut apart one of the templates to make individual house pieces. Write the numbers on the roof pieces to avoid confusion.

2 Cut out the roof pieces. Place the pattern with the wrong side up on the wrong side of the fabric. Draw the finished (sewing) line and label it with the pattern number.

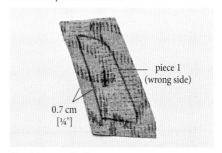

3 Add 0.7 cm [¼"] seam allowance and cut out the piece.

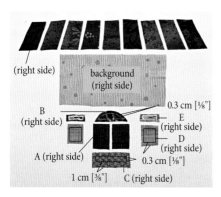

(right side)

background
(right side)

0.3 cm [⅛"]

B
(right side)

E
(right side)

D
(right side)

A (right side)

0.3 cm [⅛"]

1 cm [⅜"]   C (right side)

4 Cut nine roof pieces in the same manner. Cut out the appliqué background fabric with a 0.7 cm [¼"] seam allowance on the top edge and 1 cm [⅜"] seam allowances on the other three edges. For appliqué pieces, place patterns on the right side of the fabric, trace finished (sewing) lines, and cut out pieces with 0.3 cm [⅛"] seam allowances. Note that the two A pieces will be sewn together first and then appliquéd.

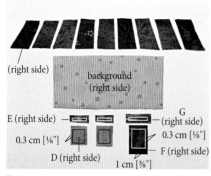

(right side)

background
(right side)

E (right side)

G
(right side)

0.3 cm [⅛"]

0.3 cm [⅛"]

D (right side)

F (right side)

1 cm [⅜"]

5 In the same manner, cut out the pieces for the pouch back.

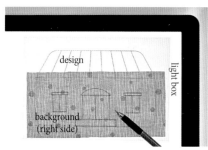

design

light box

background
(right side)

6 Trace the appliqué design on the appliqué background fabric. After placing the design on the light box and the background fabric on top of the design, use a transfer pen to trace the appliqué design onto the fabric. If you don't have a light box, you can trace on a window on a sunny day.

2. Piecing

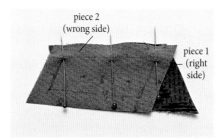

piece 2
(wrong side)

piece 1
(right side)

1 Put roof pieces 1 and 2 right sides together, and pin at both ends and the center.

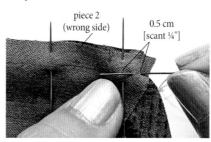

piece 2
(wrong side)

0.5 cm
[scant ¼"]

2 Make a knot at the end of the thread. Insert the needle 0.5 cm [scant ¼"] from the marked point and take one stitch.

piece 2
(wrong side)

3 Backstitch through the same holes as the first stitch.

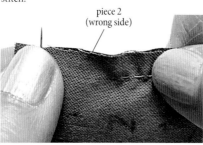

piece 2
(wrong side)

4 Sew with a running stitch.

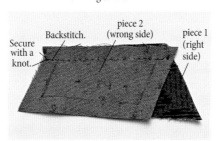

Backstitch.

piece 2
(wrong side)

piece 1
(right side)

Secure with a knot.

5 Stitch roughly 0.5 cm [scant ¼"] beyond the marked point, backstitch once, and secure with a knot.

6 Square up the edges.

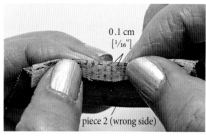

0.1 cm
[¹⁄₁₆"]

piece 2 (wrong side)

7 Fold the finished seam allowance to one side and press, leaving 0.1 cm [¹⁄₁₆"] showing over the fold. This helps hide the seam when the piece is opened up.

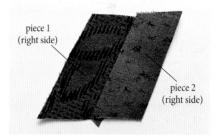

piece 1
(right side)

piece 2
(right side)

8 Turn right side out and press to smooth out any wrinkles.

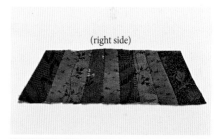

(right side)

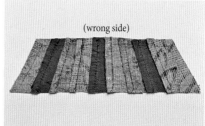

(wrong side)

9 Working in numerical order, add pieces 3 through 9 to the step 8 unit in the same manner. Press the seam allowances in one direction. In the same manner, sew together the nine roof pieces for the pouch back.

3. Appliquéing

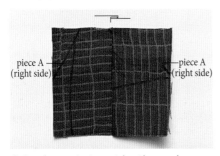

1 Sew the two A pieces right sides together; press the seam allowances to one side.

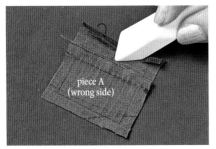

piece A (wrong side)

2 Fold the side seam allowance to the wrong side, and use the Hera marker to crease a line.

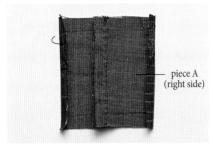

piece A (right side)

3 In the same manner, fold the seam allowance on the other side of piece A.

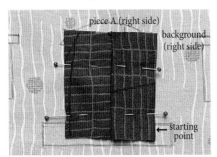

piece A (right side)

background (right side)

starting point

4 Follow the design on the background fabric and pin to secure piece A. You will start appliquéing the piece from the lower bottom edge of the right side.

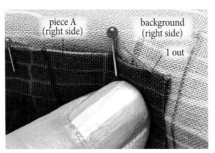

piece A (right side)

background (right side)

1 out

5 Blindstitch the appliqué pieces, making invisible stitches. First, insert the needle from the wrong side of the background fabric, and come up at the starting point (1) in the crease of piece A.

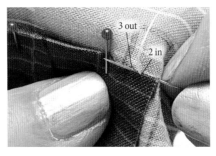

3 out

2 in

6 Insert the needle directly below the crease (2) and come up roughly 0.3 cm [⅛"] ahead on the crease (3). Repeat blindstitching (using invisible stitches; see p. 53) to secure the piece in place.

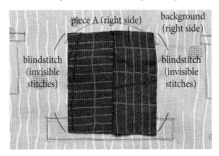

piece A (right side)

background (right side)

blindstitch (invisible stitches)

blindstitch (invisible stitches)

7 Blindstitch both sides of piece A, making invisible stitches. Do not blindstitch at the top and bottom edges, since they will be overlapped by pieces B and C.

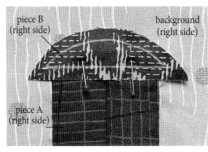

piece B (right side)

background (right side)

piece A (right side)

8 Pin piece B to the designated location.

9 Start stitching the straight line on the bottom edge. Use the needle tip to tuck under the seam allowance as you blindstitch between marks, making invisible stitches. When you come to a corner, insert needle exactly through the corner.

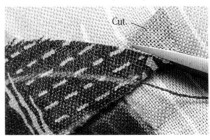

Cut.

10 Snip off the dog-ear corner.

11 To make a beautiful and sharp corner, you will need to tuck under the seam allowance three times. First use needle tip to tuck under half the width of the seam allowance to make a triangle.

12 Tuck under seam allowance one more time to make a triangle; use the needle tip to tuck under the seam allowance farther along the marked line.

13 Adjust the corner along the marked line, and blindstitch, making invisible stitches.

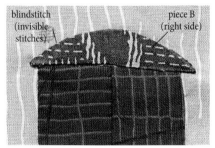

14 Continue to blindstitch, making invisible stitches as you use the needle tip to tuck under the seam allowance.

pouch front

piece E (right side)   background (right side)   piece E (right side)

piece D (right side)   piece D (right side)

Leave open.   piece C (right side)

15 Appliqué pieces C, D, and E in alphabetical order to the pouch front.

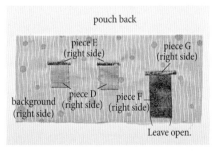

pouch back

piece E (right side)   piece G (right side)

background (right side)   piece D (right side)   piece F (right side)

Leave open.

16 In the same manner, appliqué pieces D, E, F, and G in alphabetical order to the pouch back background fabric, making invisible stitches.

4. Joining the roof and pouch and adding embroidery

See p. 53 for embroidery stitch instructions.

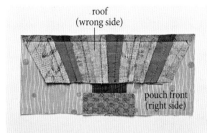

roof (wrong side)

pouch front (right side)

1 Sew the appliquéd background fabric for the pouch front and the roof right sides together.

pouch front (wrong side)

2 Press the seam allowance made in step 1 toward the roof.

pouch front (right side)

3 Hoop the sewn piece in an embroidery hoop, making sure the fabric is taut.

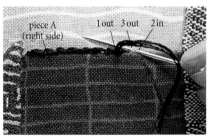

piece A (right side)   1 out 3 out 2 in

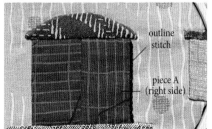

outline stitch

piece A (right side)

4 Using four strands of black embroidery floss, outline stitch along the edge of appliquéd piece A. Insert the needle from the back to start stitching, and make a knot on the back to end stitching.

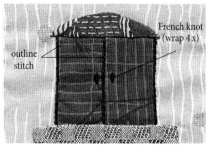

French knot (wrap 4 x)

outline stitch

5 Outline stitch along the other edge and at the center of piece A. Make a French knot (wrapped four times) with four strands of black embroidery floss for the doorknob.

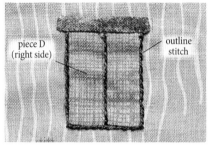

piece D (right side)   outline stitch

6 Outline stitch around the outer edges and at the center of window piece D.

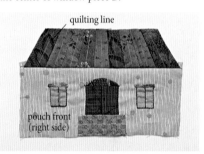

quilting line

pouch front (right side)

7 When you have embroidered the entire pouch front, use a pen to mark quilting lines between roof pieces.

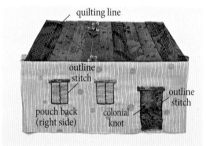

quilting line

outline stitch

pouch back (right side)   colonial knot   outline stitch

8 In the same manner, sew roof pieces together for the pouch back. Embroider, then mark quilting lines.

5. Making the quilt sandwich and basting together

1 Cut out backing and batting for the pouch front with 3 cm [1¼"] seam allowances.

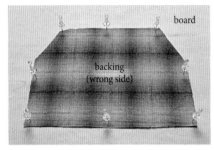

2 With the wrong side up, smooth the backing fabric out on a flat surface and pin or tape to hold it taut.

3 Place batting on the backing prepared in step 2. Smooth out the batting and keep the layers taut. Remove the push pins from the backing (secured in step 2), and put them in around the batting.

4 Put the top on the center of the layers prepared in step 3. Carefully smooth out the wrinkles and put the push pins in around the edges.

5 To baste, start in the center of the pouch with a length of knotted thread. Insert the needle from the top, and take a large stitch toward the left edge. Be sure to catch all the way to the backing. Use a spoon to help lift the needle tip from the surface as you baste. Working in the same manner, make one stitch at a time.

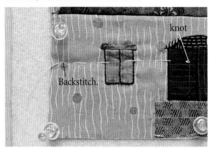

6 When you reach the edge, backstitch once at the end, leave about 2 to 3 cm [¾" to 1¼"], and trim the thread.

7 Repeat basting from the center out in a sunburst pattern following the order in the diagram above. Then baste along the seam allowance on the edges of the pouch front (15). In the same manner, make a quilt sandwich with the pouch back; baste.

6. Quilting

Starting and Finishing Quilting

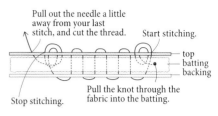

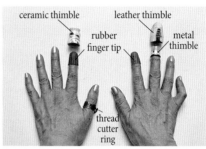

1 To protect fingers, I normally wear rubber finger tips and thimbles.

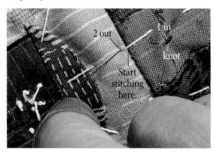

2 Quilt from the center toward the edges. Make a knot at the end of the quilting thread. Insert the needle from the top, a little away from where you plan to take the first stitch (1). Catch the batting and come up one stitch ahead of where you would like to start (2). Tug the thread to pull the knot through the fabric into the batting.

3 Take one little backstitch (3), and catch the batting. Come up at (4), which is the same spot as (2) in the previous step.

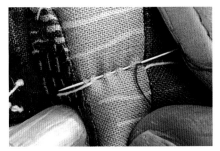

4 Take one more stitch back and insert the needle at the same spot as (3). This time catch the backing and make running stitches.

5 To end a line of quilting stitches, backstitch into the preceding space, bringing the needle up to create the final stitch.

6 Insert the needle in the last stitch again and work the needle through the batting, bringing the tip of the needle out a little away from the last stitch. Cut the thread close to the quilt top.

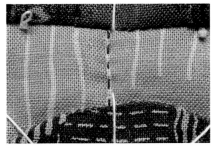

7 Now you have completed one quilting line.

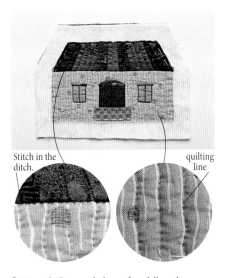

Stitch in the ditch.

quilting line

8 To quilt the pouch front, first follow the pattern of the fabric and quilt the appliqué background fabric as desired. Next, quilt the inside of the door and roof. At the end, stitch in the ditch (quilting to be added right next to seams of pieces or appliqués) along patchwork and appliqué seams. When quilting is complete, remove the basting stitches except for the ones on the outer edges.

9 Quilt the pouch back in the same manner as the pouch front.

7. Making the lower gusset

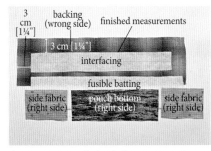

3 cm [1¼"]

backing (wrong side)

finished measurements

3 cm [1¼"]

interfacing

fusible batting

side fabric (right side)

pouch bottom (right side)

side fabric (right side)

1 Prepare materials for the lower gusset. Cut the backing with 3 cm [1¼"] seam allowances and cut the interfacing equal to the finished measurements. Press to fuse the interfacing to the wrong side of the backing. Cut the other pieces with 1 cm [⅜"] seam allowances.

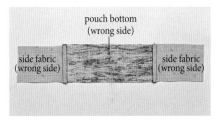

pouch bottom (wrong side)

side fabric (wrong side)

side fabric (wrong side)

2 Sew side fabric to the right and left edges of the pouch bottom fabric, right sides together. Press the seam allowances toward the pouch bottom.

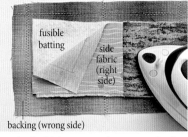

fusible batting

side fabric (right side)

backing (wrong side)

3 Put the fusible batting on the wrong side of the top prepared in step 2, and place the layers on the wrong side of the backing. Press to fuse.

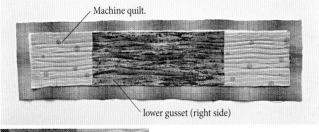

Machine quilt.

lower gusset (right side)

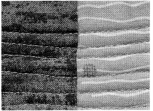

4 Machine quilt as desired, following the pattern of the fabric. Now the lower gusset is complete.

8. Making the upper gusset

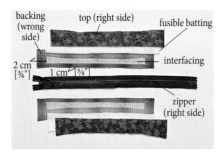

backing (wrong side) — top (right side) — fusible batting — interfacing — zipper (right side)

2 cm [¾"]   1 cm [⅜"]

1 Cut out the top, double-sided fusible batting, and backing with 1 cm [⅜"] seam allowances for edges where the zipper is installed and 2 cm [¾"] seam allowances for the other edges. Cut two pieces of each. Cut double-sided fusible interfacing even with the finished measurements, and fuse it on the wrong side of the backing.

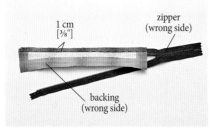

1 cm [⅜"]   zipper (wrong side)   backing (wrong side)

2 Put the backing and top right sides together, sandwiching the zipper in between (be sure to leave the zipper open). Put the fusible batting on the wrong side of the top. Sew the four layers together.

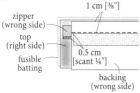

1 cm [⅜"]   zipper (wrong side)   top (right side)   fusible batting   0.5 cm [scant ¼"]   backing (wrong side)

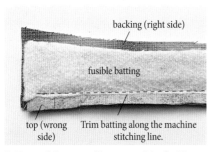

backing (right side)   fusible batting   top (wrong side)   Trim batting along the machine stitching line.

3 Trim off the seam allowances of the fusible batting along the machine stitching line.

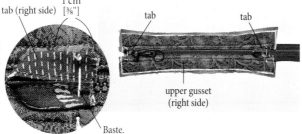

1 cm [⅜"]   tab (right side)

7 Fold the tabs prepared in step 6 in half as shown in the picture, and baste them to each end of the upper gusset prepared in Step 5.

tab   tab   upper gusset (right side)   Baste.

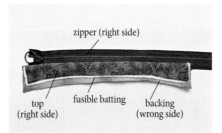

zipper (right side)   top (right side)   fusible batting   backing (wrong side)

4 Turn right side out, and press to fuse the fusible batting.

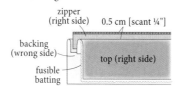

zipper (right side)   0.5 cm [scant ¼"]   backing (wrong side)   fusible batting   top (right side)

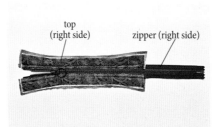

top (right side)   zipper (right side)

5 Repeat steps 2 through 4 to sew the top and backing to the other side of the zipper tape. Topstitch twice on both edges from the top.

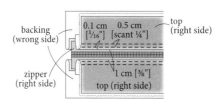

backing (wrong side)   0.1 cm [¹⁄₁₆"]   0.5 cm [scant ¼"]   top (right side)   zipper (right side)   1 cm [⅜"]   top (right side)

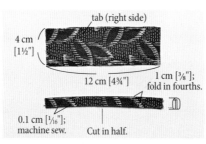

tab (right side)   4 cm [1½"]   12 cm [4¾"]   1 cm [⅜"]; fold in fourths.   0.1 cm [¹⁄₁₆"]; machine sew.   Cut in half.

6 Fold the 4 x 12 cm [1½" x 4¾"] tab in fourths to make it 1 cm [⅜"] wide. Machine sew along the folded edge. Cut the sewn tab in half.

9. Sewing the gusset and pouch

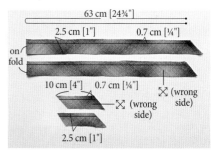

63 cm [24¾"]   2.5 cm [1"]   0.7 cm [¼"]   on fold   10 cm [4"]   0.7 cm [¼"]   (wrong side)   (wrong side)   2.5 cm [1"]

1 Cut the backing to make bias binding for seam allowances. Cut two pieces each according to the dimensions in the picture. Draw a line on the wrong side 0.7 cm [¼"] from the edge.

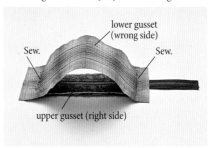

lower gusset (wrong side)   Sew.   Sew.   upper gusset (right side)

2 Put the upper and lower gussets right sides together, and sew along both edges.

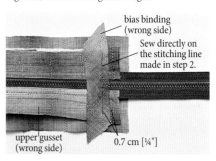

bias binding (wrong side)   Sew directly on the stitching line made in step 2.   upper gusset (wrong side)   0.7 cm [¼"]

3 Put the shorter bias binding prepared in step 1 on the wrong side of the upper gusset prepared in step 2. Match the line drawn on the bias binding with the stitching line made in step 2, and sew together.

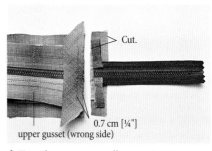

Cut.   upper gusset (wrong side)   0.7 cm [¼"]

4 Trim the gusset seam allowance to 0.7 cm [¼"] wide.

5 Bind the gusset seam allowance with bias binding. (Use a stiletto to help push the bias strip in place over the thick seam allowance.)

6 Press the seam allowance prepared in step 5 toward the lower gusset and blindstitch.

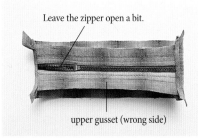

7 Repeat steps 3 through 6 to stitch the other edges of the upper and lower gussets to make a gusset loop. Be sure to leave the zipper open somewhat.

8 Use the basting stitches around the outer edges to position the pattern on the wrong side of the quilted pouch front. Trace finished (sewing) lines and mark points to match. Do the same for the pouch back.

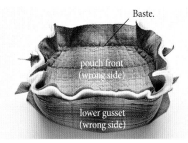

9 Put the pouch front prepared in step 8 and the gusset prepared in step 7 right sides together, match the marked points, and baste all around.

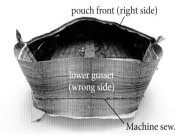

10 Machine sew along the basting stitches made in step 9, and remove the basting stitches.

11 In the same manner, put the pouch back and the other side of the gusset right sides together. Baste and machine sew.

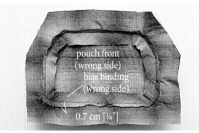

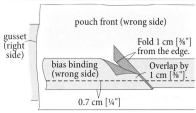

12 Match the machine stitching line made in step 10 with the line drawn on the bias binding (0.7 cm [¼"] from the edge), right sides together. Machine sew directly on the stitching line. As shown in the figure above, fold the start of the bias binding 1 cm [⅜"] from the edge. Overlap the end of the bias binding by 1 cm [⅜"] with the start of the bias binding. Trim away the excess bias binding.

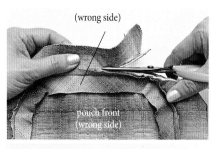

13 Trim the pouch front and gusset even with the bias binding seam allowance. In the same manner, sew the bias binding onto the pouch back, and trim off the seam allowances.

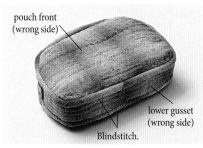

14 Bind the seam allowance with the bias binding, press toward the gusset, and blindstitch.

15 Turn right side out and smooth out the wrinkles. The pouch is now complete.

Simple Silhouette Bag shown on p. 6

A   B   C

Materials for A

Cottons
- Gray stripe - 40 x 35 cm [16" x 14"] (bag front background, pieces E and F, handle)
- Black woven homespun - 35 x 35 cm [14" x 14"] (bag back, handle)
- Dark gray print - 20 x 25 cm [8" x 10"] (pieces A, B, and C)
- Green - 5 x 7 cm [2" x 3"] (piece D)

Interfacing - 15 x 20 cm [6" x 8"] (piece C)
Embroidery floss: black and green

Materials for B

Cottons
- Beige check - 40 x 35 cm [16" x 14"] (bag front background, pieces B and C, handle)
- Beige woven homespun - 35 x 35 cm [14" x 14"] (bag back, handle)
- Brown check - 25 x 17 cm [10" x 7"] (piece A)

Interfacing - 25 x 15 cm [10" x 6"] (piece A)
Embroidery floss: black

Materials for C

Cottons
- Gray print - 40 x 35 cm [16" x 14"] (bag front background, piece C, handle)
- Light brown woven homespun - 35 x 35 cm [14" x 14"] (bag back, handle)
- Navy blue check - 18 x 23 cm [8" x 10"] (pieces A and B)

Interfacing - 13 x 21 cm [6" x 9"] (piece B)
Embroidery floss: black and navy blue

Making A

1 Referring to dimensional diagram A above right and the full-size template on side D of the pattern sheet inserts, trace the appliqué design onto the right side of appliqué piece C. Cut interfacing to the finished measurements (do not include seam allowances) and fuse it to the wrong side of appliqué piece C. Appliqué pieces D, E, and F onto piece C, making invisible stitches, and stitch embroideries. Trace the design onto the bag front background fabric. Appliqué pieces A, B, and C in alphabetical order (figure 1).

2 To make the handles, fold the handle fabric in half lengthwise, right sides together, and sew 2 cm [¾"] from the folded edge. Center the seam and press open. Use a tube turner to turn right side out. Sew along both folded edges (figure 2). Make two.

3 Put the bag front and back pieces right sides together, and sew along both sides and bottom edges. Fold the excess seam allowance on the bag back over the seam allowance on the bag front, and machine sew to bind the edges (figure 3).

4 Fold under the seam allowance on the top edge of the bag twice to 2.5 cm [1"] wide, and press. Put the bag handles on the bag front and back. Tuck the ends of the bag handle under the bag opening. Topstitch along both edges of the 2.5 cm [1"] bag opening. Turn right side out and smooth out wrinkles (figure 4).

Finished measurements for each bag

- Length (l): 25 cm [9¾"]; width (w): 23 cm [9"]
- The full-size template/pattern can be found on side D of the pattern sheet inserts.

Dimensional Diagram B

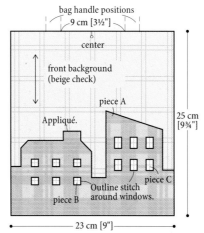

Making B and C

Although appliqué designs are different, bags B and C are made in the same manner as bag A.

Dimensional Diagram A

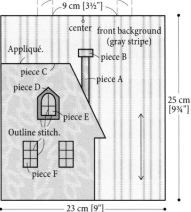

Dimensional Diagram C

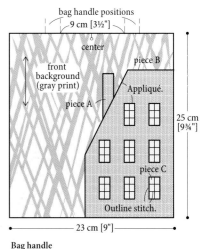

- When cutting the bag front (background), add a 3.5 cm [1⅜"] seam allowance to the top edge, and add 0.7 cm [¼"] seam allowances to the other three edges. Cut the bag back with a 3.5 cm [1⅜"] seam allowance on the top edge and 2 cm [¾"] seam allowances on the other three edges.
- When cutting appliqués, add 0.3 to 0.4 cm [⅛"] seam allowances. Cut handles with 1 cm [⅜"] seam allowances.

Figure 1: Appliquéing

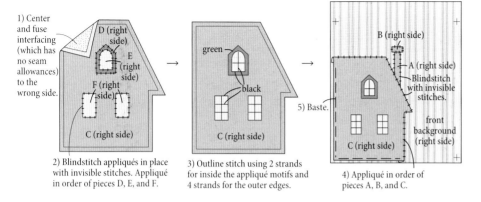

1) Center and fuse interfacing (which has no seam allowances) to the wrong side.

D (right side)
E (right side)
F (right side)
C (right side)

2) Blindstitch appliqués in place with invisible stitches. Appliqué in order of pieces D, E, and F.

green
black
C (right side)

3) Outline stitch using 2 strands for inside the appliqué motifs and 4 strands for the outer edges.

5) Baste.

B (right side)
A (right side)
Blindstitch with invisible stitches.
front background (right side)
C (right side)

4) Appliqué in order of pieces A, B, and C.

Figure 2: Making handles

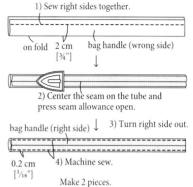

1) Sew right sides together.
on fold 2 cm [¾"] bag handle (wrong side)

2) Center the seam on the tube and press seam allowance open.

bag handle (right side) 3) Turn right side out.

0.2 cm [¹/₁₆"] 4) Machine sew.

Make 2 pieces.

Figure 3: Sewing bag front and back together

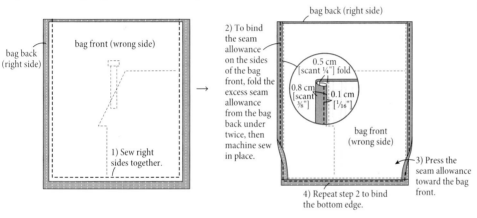

bag back (right side)
bag front (wrong side)

1) Sew right sides together.

bag back (right side)

2) To bind the seam allowance on the sides of the bag front, fold the excess seam allowance from the bag back under twice, then machine sew in place.

0.5 cm [scant ¼"] fold
0.8 cm [scant ³/₈"]
0.1 cm [¹/₁₆"]
bag front (wrong side)

3) Press the seam allowance toward the bag front.

4) Repeat step 2 to bind the bottom edge.

Figure 4: Sewing bag's top edge and attaching bag handles

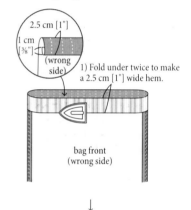

2.5 cm [1"]
1 cm [³/₈"]
(wrong side)

1) Fold under twice to make a 2.5 cm [1"] wide hem.

bag front (wrong side)

bag handle (bag back)
bag handle (front)

2) Put the bag handle on top; machine sew.

0.2 cm [¹/₁₆"]

Tuck under the bag opening by 1 cm [³/₈"].

0.2 cm [¹/₁₆"]

bag front (wrong side)

Finished Bags

A

B

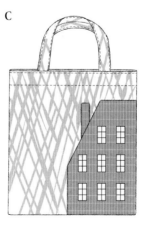

C

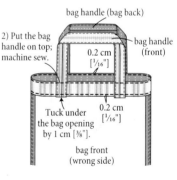

Village Tote
shown on p. 8

Finished Measurements
- Length (l): 31 cm [12¼"]; width (w): 28 cm [11"]; gusset width: 9 cm [3½"]
- The bag front template/pattern can be found on side A of the pattern sheet inserts.

Materials Needed
Cottons
- Assorted fat quarters or scraps (approximately 45 pieces) as needed for patchwork
- Plaid A - 45 x 95 cm [18" x 38"] (bag front opening, bag back, gusset, handle top, bias binding for bag opening)
- Plaid B - 55 x 100 cm [22" x 40"] (backing)

Batting - 55 x 100 cm [22" x 40"]

Heavyweight interfacing - 10 x 90 cm [4" x 36"] (gusset)

Lightweight interfacing - 5 x 30 cm [2" x 12"] (handles)

Woven cotton webbing - 3 x 60 cm [1¼" x 24"] (handles)

Instructions
1 Using the bag front template/pattern on side A of the pattern sheet inserts, make 12 house blocks for the bag front and sew together. Press seams in opposing directions to reduce bulk. Sew the opening to the bag top edge (figure 1).

2 Make a quilt sandwich with the top, batting, and backing for the bag front and the bag back. Baste and quilt. Draw finished (sewing) lines on the backing but do not trim batting or backing yet.

3 Machine sew the plaid A handle top to the bag handle webbing to make a bag handle. Make two handles (figure 2).

4 Sandwich one bag handle between the bag front and one bias binding strip. Sew. Bind the edges with the bias binding strip cut for the bag opening. Repeat to sew the other handle between the bag back and the remaining bias binding strip (figure 3).

5 To make the gusset, fuse the heavyweight interfacing on the wrong side of the gusset backing. Put the gusset top and backing right sides together. Put the batting on the wrong side of the gusset top. Sew right along the interfacing on the short edges. Trim batting close to seams, turn right side out, and machine quilt. Draw finished (sewing) lines on the backing and mark the points to match (figure 4).

6 Sew the bag and gusset right sides together. Use the gusset backing to bind the seam allowances. Turn right side out and smooth out wrinkles (figure 5).

Dimensional Diagram

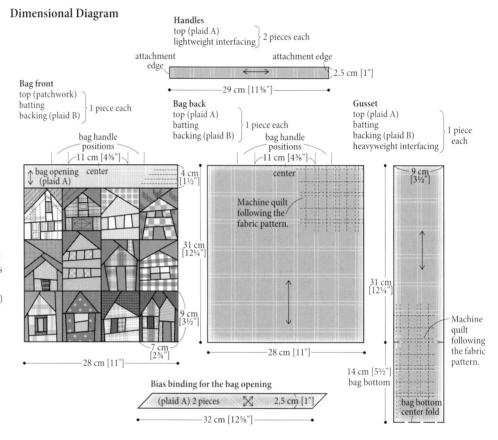

When cutting, do not add seam allowance to the following: attachment edges on the handle fabric, lightweight interfacing, heavyweight interfacing for the gusset, and bias binding for the bag opening. Cut out the backing and batting adding 3 cm [1¼"] seam allowances. Cut out all other pieces adding 0.7 cm [¼"] seam allowances.

Figure 1: Sewing bag front top pieces together

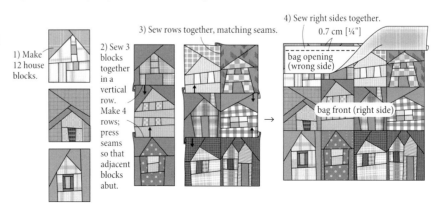

Figure 2: Making handles

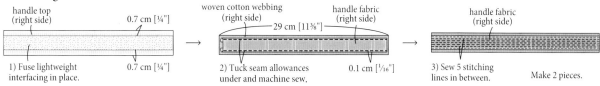

handle top (right side)   0.7 cm [¼"]

1) Fuse lightweight interfacing in place.   0.7 cm [¼"]

woven cotton webbing (right side)   handle fabric (right side)

29 cm [11⅜"]

2) Tuck seam allowances under and machine sew.   0.1 cm [¹⁄₁₆"]

handle fabric (right side)

3) Sew 5 stitching lines in between.   Make 2 pieces.

Figure 3: Binding the bag opening and attaching handles

bag handle (wrong side)

1) Baste the bag handle in place.

11 cm [4⅜"]

backing (wrong side)

batting

bag front (right side)

bias binding for bag opening (wrong side)

2) Sew right sides together.   0.7 cm [¼"]

bag front (right side)

3) Trim batting and backing even with edge of bias binding strip.

bag front (right side)

bag handle (right side)

bias binding (right side)   1 cm [⅜"]

4) Bind seam allowance with bias binding strip. Press toward the backing and blindstitch in place.

bag front backing (wrong side)

Make the bag back in the same manner.

bias binding

bag

Figure 4: Making the gusset

4) Cut batting along the stitching line.

3) Trim off excess backing seam allowance to 0.7 cm [¼"] from the seam.

gusset top (wrong side)

2) Sew between marked points.   0.1 cm [¹⁄₁₆"]   gusset backing (right side)

batting

gusset backing (wrong side)

3 cm [1¼"]

1) Fuse heavyweight interfacing to wrong side of the backing.

3 cm [1¼"] seam allowance

2) Sew between marked points.

5) Turn right side out and machine quilt following the fabric pattern.

backing   batting

gusset top (right side)

6) Draw finished (sewing) lines on the wrong side. Measure and mark points as shown.

31 cm [12¼"]   28 cm [11"]   31 cm [12¼"]

gusset backing (right side)

Figure 5: Sewing the bag and gusset together

gusset (right side)

right sides together

3) Trim all seam allowances (except gusset backing) to 0.7 cm [¼"].

1) Sew up to the marked point on the corner, right sides together.

gusset backing seam allowance (wrong side)

bag front backing (right side)

2) Sew between the corners.

4) Use the gusset backing to bind the seam allowances; blindstitch.

gusset backing (right side)

(1)

In the same manner, sew together the bag back and gusset.

Finished Bag

bag front (right side)

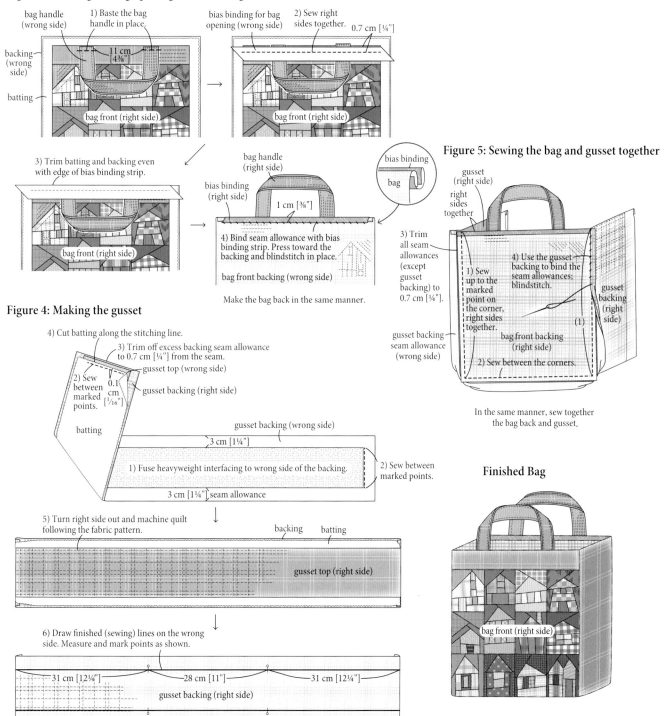

City Skyline Wall Hanging shown on p. 10

Finished Measurements

- Length (l): 33 cm [13"]; width (w): 108 cm [42½"]
- The template/pattern can be found on side A of the pattern sheet inserts.

Materials Needed

Cottons
- Assorted fat quarters or scraps (approx. 95 pieces) as needed for appliqués
- Print - 105 x 30 cm [42" x 12"] (background fabric)
- Woven stripe - 40 x 110 cm [16" x 44"] (border)
- Woven check - 155 x 45 cm [62" x 18"] (backing, bias binding for seam allowances)

Batting - 120 x 40 cm [48" x 16"]

Embroidery floss: brown, dark brown, silver gray, dark gray, gray, ecru, smoky pink, salmon pink, green, mustard, blue, black

Instructions

1 Referring to dimensional diagram and figure 1 below, and the full-size template on side A of the pattern sheet inserts, trace design onto background fabric, blindstitch appliqué pieces, and embroider.

2 Sew short border strips to right and left sides of background fabric prepared in step 1. Trim seam allowances 0.7 cm [¼"] from the seam, and press the seam allowances toward the border.

3 Sew long border strips to top and bottom edges of the background fabric. Press seam allowances toward border to complete quilt top.

4 Make a quilt sandwich with quilt top, batting, and backing. Baste and quilt (see dimensional diagram).

5 Use a 2.5 cm [1"] wide bias strip to bind the quilt edges (figure 2). (For a graphic finish to the wall hanging, the seam allowances and binding are pressed completely toward the backing.)

Dimensional Diagram

Wall hanging
top (pieced, appliquéd, and embroidered)
batting
backing (woven check) } 1 piece each

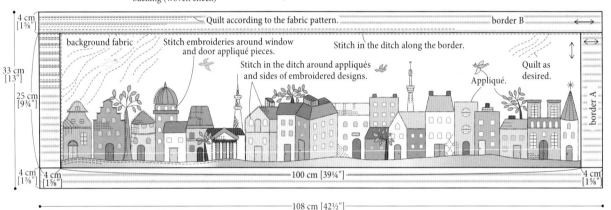

When cutting, add 0.4 cm [⅛"] seam allowances to appliqué fabrics, 1 cm [⅜"] seam allowances to borders A and B, and 3 cm [1¼"] seam allowances to batting and backing. Cut 2 pieces each of bias binding (2.5 x 35 cm [1" x 13¾"] and 2.5 x 110 cm [1" x 43⅜"]) from check fabric for binding seam allowances.

Figure 1: Appliquéing   Figure 2: Binding seam allowances

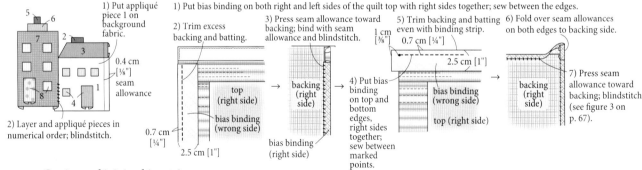

Cutting and joining bias strips

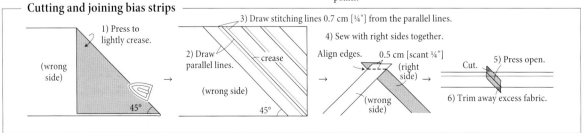

Pencil Case shown on p. 12

Finished Measurements
- Length (l): approx. 5 cm [2"]; opening width: 16.5 cm [6½"]
- The template/pattern can be found on side C of the pattern sheet inserts.

Materials Needed
Cottons
- Blue-and-brown check - 20 x 13 cm [8" x 6"] (case front and back)
- Moss green check - 20 x 8 cm [8" x 4"] (case bottom)
- Brown check - 16 x 6 cm [7" x 3"] (gusset)
- Assorted fat quarters or scraps (11 pieces) as needed for appliqués
- Gray print - 27 x 16 cm [11" x 7"] (backing)
Double-sided fusible batting - 20 x 16 cm [8" x 3"]
Metal clasp purse frame - 16.5 x 3.5 cm [6½" x 1⅜"]
Thin paper string or twine - 50 cm [20"]
Embroidery floss: red, brown, dark brown, blue, dark gray, silver gray, yellow-green, green, black
Craft glue

Instructions
1 Referring to the dimensional diagram above right and the full-size template on side C of the pattern sheet inserts, blindstitch appliqué pieces 1 to 11 in numerical order to case front background fabric, making invisible stitches. Stitch the embroidered details. Then appliqué and embroider the case back background fabric in the same manner.
2 Sew case front and back pieces to top and bottom edges of the case bottom, respectively. Press the seam allowances toward the case bottom.
3 Put the case top (prepared in step 2) and backing right sides together. Put the fusible batting on the wrong side of the backing. Sew all around, leaving an opening to turn right side out. Trim off excess batting, turn right side out, and blindstitch to close the opening. Press to fuse the batting in place (figure 1).
4 In the same manner as step 3, sew the gusset top, backing, and fusible batting together. Turn right side out and smooth out the wrinkles.
5 With right sides together, match centers of case and one gusset; match marks on gusset to seams on case. Whipstitch top layers together. Next, ladder stitch to sew the backing layers together (see steps 1 and 2 of figure 2 on p. 76 for visuals of this process). Repeat to sew the remaining gusset to the other end of the case.
6 Turn right side out, and attach the metal clasp purse frame (figure 2).

Dimensional Diagram

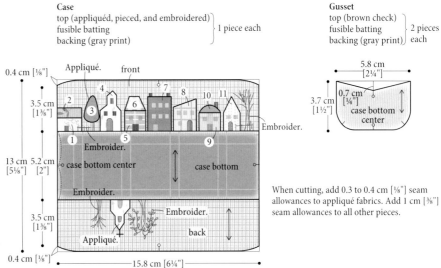

Case
top (appliquéd, pieced, and embroidered)
fusible batting
backing (gray print) } 1 piece each

Gusset
top (brown check)
fusible batting
backing (gray print) } 2 pieces each

When cutting, add 0.3 to 0.4 cm [⅛"] seam allowances to appliqué fabrics. Add 1 cm [⅜"] seam allowances to all other pieces.

Figure 1: Sewing case pieces

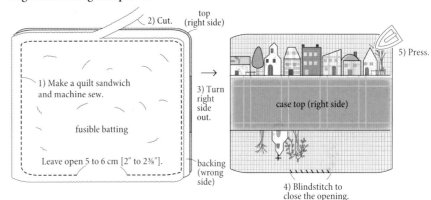

Figure 2: Installing the metal clasp

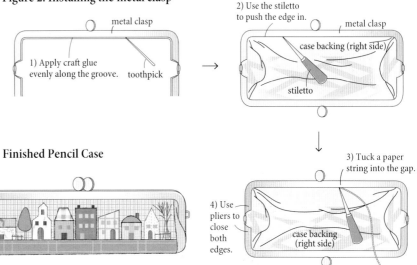

Before using pliers, be sure to put a piece of fabric on the metal clasp to protect it from tool marks.

Finished Pencil Case

Spring • Summer • Autumn • Winter shown on p. 14

Spring   Summer   Autumn   Winter

Finished Measurements (same frame dimensions for all 4 projects)
- Frame dimensions: 9 x 9 cm [3½" x 3½"] (inside); 14.8 x 14.8 cm [5⅞" x 5⅞"] (outside)
- The templates/patterns can be found on side A of the pattern sheet inserts.

Materials Needed for Spring
Cottons
- Beige leaf print - 15 x 12 cm [6" x 5"] (background fabric)
- Blue-and-green stripe - 6 x 6 cm [3" x 3"] (piece 1)
- Dark gray print - 2 x 4 cm [1" x 2"] (piece 2)
- Brown print - 8 x 8 cm [4" x 4"] (pieces 3 and 6)
- Gray lattice print - 6 x 4 cm [3" x 2"] (piece 4)
- Gray stripe - 4 x 4 cm [2" x 2"] (piece 5)
- Beige-and-blue lattice print - 10 x 10 cm [4" x 4"] (piece 7)
- Gray print - 15 x 6 cm [6" x 3"] (piece 8)
- Light-gray-and-aqua lattice print - 5 x 5 cm [2" x 2"] (piece 9)

Batting - 15 x 15 cm [6" x 6"]
Embroidery floss: blue, light green, orange
Painter's tape
Dark brown frame

Materials Needed for Summer
Cottons
- Black - 15 x 15 cm [6" x 6"] (background fabric)
- Dark brown print - 10 x 10 cm [4" x 4"] (piece 2)
- Orange print - 2 x 2 cm [1" x 1"] (piece 1)
- Red-and-brown print - 7 x 7 cm [3" x 3"] (piece 3)
- Green print - 7 x 7 cm [3" x 3"] (piece 4)
- Sand print - 3 x 3 cm [2" x 2"] (piece 5)

Batting - 15 x 15 cm [6" x 6"]
Embroidery floss: silver gray, dark brown, yellow
Painter's tape
Dark brown frame

Materials Needed for Autumn
Cottons
- Beige print - 15 x 15 cm [6" x 6"] (background fabric)
- Dark gray print - 4 x 7 cm [2" x 3"] (piece 1)
- Brown print - 2.5 x 7 cm [1" x 3"] (piece 2)
- Light brown lattice print - 7 x 7 cm [3" x 3"] (piece 3)
- Dark green print - 4 x 4 cm [2" x 2"] (piece 4)
- Gray print - 4 x 5 cm [1¾" x 2"] (piece 5)
- Brown lattice print - 4 x 5 cm [1¾" x 2"] (piece 6)
- Red-and-brown print - 1.5 x 3 cm [1" x 2"] (piece 7)

Batting - 15 x 15 cm [6" x 6"]
Embroidery floss: brown, light gray, black
Painter's tape
Dark brown frame

Materials Needed for Winter
Cottons
- Light gray print - 15 x 15 cm [6" x 6"] (background fabric)
- Red lattice print - 9 x 6 cm [4" x 3"] (piece 4)
- Dark gray print - 3 x 3 cm [2" x 2"] (piece 1)
- Dark brown print - 9 x 9 cm [4" x 4"] (piece 6)
- White print - 9 x 9 cm [4" x 4"] (piece 7)
- Blue print A - 5 x 3 cm [2" x 1¼"] (piece 5)
- Red stripe - 5 x 9 cm [2" x 4"] (piece 2)
- Blue print B - 5 x 4 cm [2" x 1¾"] (piece 3)

Batting - 15 x 15 cm [6" x 6"]
Embroidery floss: white, cream, black
Painter's tape
Dark brown frame

Instructions (same for all 4 projects)
1 When cutting appliqués, add 0.3 to 0.4 cm [⅛"] seam allowances to most edges. However, on any appliqué edge that is on the outer edge of the background, add 1.5 to 2 cm [⅝" to ¾"] seam allowances to those edges. Cut out the background fabric with 3 cm [1⅛"] seam allowances.

2 Using the template and dimensional diagram, which are both on side A of the pattern sheet inserts, trace the template and design onto the background fabric.

3 First sew together the patchwork pieces. Then blindstitch the joined patchwork to the background fabric, making invisible stitches. Stitch embroideries (see the template).

4 Put the batting on the wrong side. Fold the edges of your work over the frame mount board. Use the painter's tape to secure. Put your work in the frame.

Flat Pouch

shown on p. 44

Finished Measurements

- Length (l): 16.2 cm [6⅜"]; opening width: 11.4 cm [4½"]
- The template/pattern can be found on side C of the pattern sheet inserts.

Materials Needed

Cottons

- Assorted fat quarters or scraps (7 pieces) (patchwork)
- Woven homespun A - 5 x 6 cm [2" x 3"] (loop)
- Black check - 3.5 cm [1⅜"] wide bias tape (20 cm) [8"] (binding for pouch bottom)
- Woven homespun B - 30 x 20 cm [12" x 8"] (backing, fabric to bind zipper tape end)

Batting - 30 x 20 cm [12" x 8"]

Zipper - 20 cm [8"] long

O-ring - 3.2 cm [1¼"] outer diameter

Instructions

1 Make the loop (figure 1).

2 Referring to the dimensional diagram above right and the full-size template on side C of the pattern sheet inserts, assemble patchwork pieces to make the pouch front top and back top.

3 Put the pouch front top and backing right sides together. Put the batting on the wrong side of the backing. Sew around the edges, leaving the bottom open to turn right side out. Repeat to make the pouch back top. Trim off the excess batting. Turn right side out, baste, and quilt in the ditch (figure 2, steps 1 and 2).

4 Put the pouch front and back right sides together. First whipstitch to sew the top pieces together, leaving open the area where you will install the zipper. Next, use a ladder stitch to sew the backing pieces together (see steps 1 and 2 of figure 2 on p. 76 for visuals of this process). Open the zipper and turn under the top edge of the zipper tape. Using a backstitch, sew the zipper to the backing of the pouch front and back (the stitches should not show on the right side of the pouch). Blindstitch the zipper tape edges to the backing, then cover the top zipper end with a facing (figure 2, steps 3 to 6).

5 Use the 3.5 cm [1⅜"] wide strip to bind the pouch bottom seam allowances (figure 3).

Dimensional Diagram

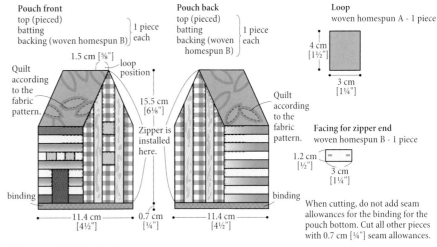

Pouch front
top (pieced)
batting
backing (woven homespun B) ⎫ 1 piece each

1.5 cm [⅝"]
loop position

Quilt according to the fabric pattern.

Pouch back
top (pieced)
batting
backing (woven homespun B) ⎫ 1 piece each

15.5 cm [6⅛"]

Zipper is installed here.

Quilt according to the fabric pattern.

binding

binding

11.4 cm [4½"]   0.7 cm [¼"]   11.4 cm [4½"]

Loop
woven homespun A - 1 piece

4 cm [1½"]
3 cm [1¼"]

Facing for zipper end
woven homespun B - 1 piece

1.2 cm [½"]
3 cm [1¼"]

When cutting, do not add seam allowances for the binding for the pouch bottom. Cut all other pieces with 0.7 cm [¼"] seam allowances.

Figure 1: Making the loop

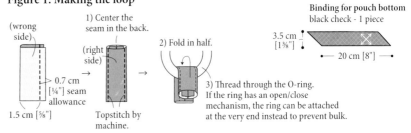

(wrong side)

1) Center the seam in the back.

(right side)

2) Fold in half.

0.7 cm [¼"] seam allowance

1.5 cm [⅝"]

Topstitch by machine.

3) Thread through the O-ring. If the ring has an open/close mechanism, the ring can be attached at the very end instead to prevent bulk.

Binding for pouch bottom
black check - 1 piece

3.5 cm [1⅜"]
20 cm [8"]

Figure 2: Making the pouch front and back and installing the zipper

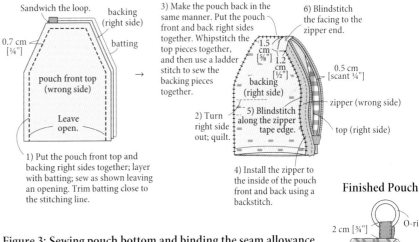

Sandwich the loop.

backing (right side)

0.7 cm [¼"]

batting

pouch front top (wrong side)

Leave open.

1) Put the pouch front top and backing right sides together; layer with batting; sew as shown leaving an opening. Trim batting close to the stitching line.

3) Make the pouch back in the same manner. Put the pouch front and back right sides together. Whipstitch the top pieces together, and then use a ladder stitch to sew the backing pieces together.

6) Blindstitch the facing to the zipper end.

1.5 cm [⅝"]
1.2 cm [½"]

backing (right side)

2) Turn right side out; quilt.

5) Blindstitch along the zipper tape edge.

4) Install the zipper to the inside of the pouch front and back using a backstitch.

0.5 cm [scant ¼"]

zipper (wrong side)

top (right side)

Finished Pouch

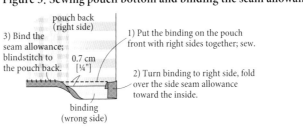

2 cm [¾"]
O-ring

0.7 cm [¼"] wide binding

Figure 3: Sewing pouch bottom and binding the seam allowance

pouch back (right side)

3) Bind the seam allowance; blindstitch to the pouch back.

0.7 cm [¼"]

1) Put the binding on the pouch front with right sides together; sew.

2) Turn binding to right side, fold over the side seam allowance toward the inside.

binding (wrong side)

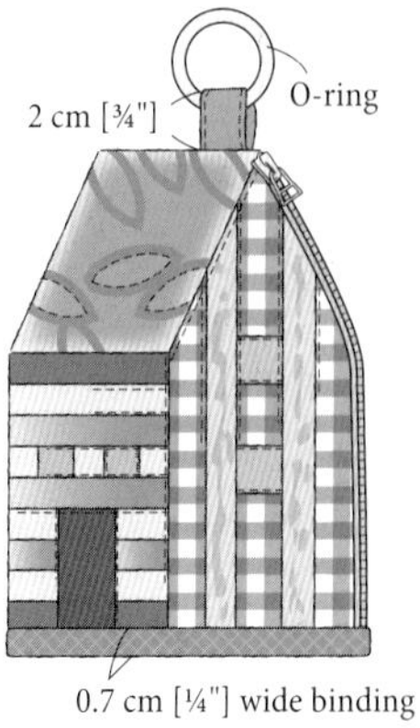

Boston Bag

shown on p. 18

Finished Measurements

- Length (l): 22.2 cm [8¾"]; width (w): 32.5 cm [12¾"]; gusset width: 6 cm [2⅜"]
- The bag front template/pattern can be found on side C of the pattern sheet inserts.

Materials Needed

Cottons

- Assorted fat quarters or scraps (approx. 30 pieces) (patchwork)
- Check A - 110 x 25 cm [44" x 10"] (bag back, gussets A and B)
- Check B - 40 x 35 cm [16" x 14"] (outer pocket)
- Woven homespun C - 10 x 90 cm [4" x 36"] (handle)
- Woven homespun D - 20 x 10 cm [8" x 4"] (tabs)
- Woven homespun E - 65 x 90 cm [26" x 36"] (backing, inner pocket, bias binding for seam allowances)

Batting - 80 x 60 cm [32" x 24"]

Heavyweight interfacing - 60 x 6 cm [24" x 3"] (gusset B)

Lightweight interfacing - 90 x 10 cm [36" x 4"] (gusset A, handles)

Double-sided fusible web - 35 x 35 cm [14" x 14"] (outer and inner pockets)

Zipper - 44 cm [17⅜"] long

Woven linen tape - 2.5 x 180 cm [1" x 71"] (handles)

Beads (0.7 cm [¼"] in diameter; 2 cm [¾"] long) - 2 pieces (large enough to thread the waxed cord through for zipper pull)

Waxed cord - 0.3 cm [⅛"] in thickness (zipper pull)

Embroidery floss: brown, gray, dark gray

Instructions

1 Machine sew the handle fabric to the woven linen tape. Make two bag handles (figure 1).

2 Referring to the dimensional diagram above right and the full-size template on side C of the pattern sheet inserts, assemble patchwork pieces to make the bag front top, and stitch embroideries (figure 2). Make a quilt sandwich with the top, batting, and backing. Baste and quilt, then trim edges even with the top.

3 Referring to the dimensional diagram, make a quilt sandwich with the bag back top, backing, and batting. Machine quilt.

4 Make the outer and inner pockets (figure 3).

5 Put the outer pocket and inner pocket on the designated locations on the right and wrong sides of the bag back. Fold the inner pocket edges out

of the way and sew the bag handle onto the bag back, making sure that the inner pocket is not caught in the stitches (figure 4). In the same manner, sew the bag handle onto the bag front.

6 Make gusset A (see p. 62). Make tabs and baste them onto both edges of gusset A (figure 5).

Dimensional Diagram

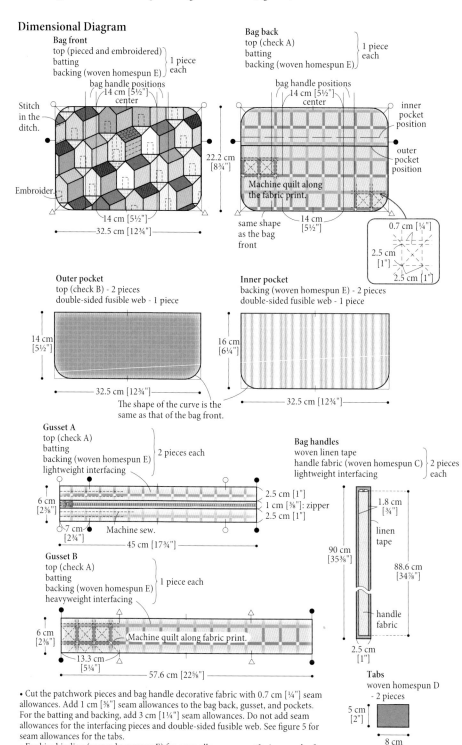

- Cut the patchwork pieces and bag handle decorative fabric with 0.7 cm [¼"] seam allowances. Add 1 cm [⅜"] seam allowances to the bag back, gusset, and pockets. For the batting and backing, add 3 cm [1¼"] seam allowances. Do not add seam allowances for the interfacing pieces and double-sided fusible web. See figure 5 for seam allowances for the tabs.
- For bias binding (woven homespun E) for seam allowances, cut 2 pieces each of 2.5 x 107 cm [1" x 42⅛"] (sewing pieces together as necessary to make a strip that long) and 2.5 x 8 cm [1" x 3⅛"].

7 Fuse heavyweight interfacing on the wrong side of the backing for gusset B. Make a quilt sandwich and machine quilt referring to the dimensional diagram.

8 Sew gussets A and B right sides together to make a loop. Use the 2.5 cm [1"] wide bias strip to bind the seam allowances, press toward gusset B, and blindstitch (figure 6).

9 Sew the bag front, bag back, and gusset prepared in step 8 right sides together. Use the 2.5 cm [1"] wide bias strip to bind the seam allowances, press toward the bag, and blindstitch. Attach the zipper pull (figure 7).

Figure 1: Making bag handles

2) Tuck under seam allowances.
0.7 cm [¼"]
1) Attach lightweight interfacing to wrong side of the handle fabric.
handle fabric (right side)
2.5 cm [1"]
1.8 cm [¾"]
woven linen tape (right side)
3) Topstitch by machine.
4) Machine sew along the center.

Figure 2: Piecing

A
0.7 cm [¼"] seam allowance
B
C (wrong side)
D
Stitch between the marked points.
Sew together pieces A to D in alphabetical order.

Figure 3: Making outer and inner pockets

1) Put outer pocket pieces right sides together; sew along the opening.
outer pocket (wrong side)
(right side)
3) Topstitch by machine.
(right side)
double-sided fusible web
2) Turn right side out; insert the double-sided fusible web; fuse.

Make the inner pocket in the same manner.

Figure 4: Making inner and outer pockets and attaching bag handles

bag back backing (right side)
inner pocket (right side)
1) Put the inner pocket on top; machine sew a dividing line along the center.

bag handle (right side)
1 cm [⅜"]
2 cm [¾"]
bag back top (right side)
outer pocket (right side)
2) Topstitch by machine, making sure inner pocket is not caught in stitching.
Layer the outer pocket and bag handle.
Fold inner pocket edges out of the way.
3) Baste the bag handle in place. Smooth out the inner pocket and put it on top; baste around the edges within the seam allowance.

Figure 5: Making and attaching tabs

0.7 cm [¼"]
1 cm [⅜"] seam allowance
(wrong side)
0.7 cm [¼"] seam allowance
1 cm [⅜"]
(wrong side)
1 cm [⅜"]
4 cm [1½"]
Center seam and press open.
(right side)
Fold in half.
2.5 cm [1"]

gusset A (right side)
on fold
Baste.
tab
tab

Figure 6: Sewing gussets A and B together

gusset A (wrong side)
2.5 cm [1"]
(wrong side)
0.7 cm [¼"]
gusset B (wrong side)
2) Put the 2.5 cm [1"] wide bias strip on top, right sides together; sew directly on the seam created in step 1.
1) Put right sides together; sew to make a loop.
3) Fold bias strip over seam allowances; blindstitch.
gusset B (wrong side)

Figure 7: Sewing the bag and gusset together

Be sure to leave the zipper open.
gusset A (wrong side)
2) Bind the seam allowances with the 2.5 cm [1"] wide bias binding strip.
bag front (wrong side)
0.7 cm [¼"]
gusset B (wrong side)
1) Put the bag and gusset right sides together; sew all around.
bias strip (wrong side)

Finished Bag

Decorative zipper pull
zipper pull
waxed cord
bead

Bread Basket shown on p. 22

Finished Measurements

- Front piece length (l): 12 cm [4¾"]; side piece length (l): 6.5 cm [2½"]; basket bottom: 14 x 10 cm [5½" x 3⅞"]
- The template/pattern can be found on side C of the pattern sheet inserts.

Materials Needed

Cottons
- Green check - 40 x 20 cm [16" x 8"] (pieces A, C, D, and F)
- Blue-gray stripe - 20 x 15 cm [8" x 6"] (piece B)
- Dark brown check - 18 x 25 cm [8" x 10"] (pieces E and G, basket bottom)
- Yellow plaid - 10 x 7 cm [4" x 3"] (window appliqués)
- Dark blue check - 10 x 4 cm [4" x 2"] (door appliqués)
- Yellow print - 50 x 25 cm [20" x 10"] (backing)

Fusible fleece or single-sided fusible batting - 50 x 25 cm [20" x 10"]

Interfacing - 50 x 25 cm [20" x 10"]

Template plastic - 50 x 25 cm [20" x 10"]

Embroidery floss: green

Instructions

1 Referring to the dimensional diagram and figure 1 at right and the full-size template on side C of the pattern sheet inserts, sew together pieces A, B, C, and D for the basket front. Do not sew into the seam allowances at the top of pieces A, C, and D.

2 Blindstitch appliqué pieces onto the right side of the front piece prepared in step 1, making invisible stitches. Stitch window embroideries (figure 2).

3 Sew the front piece prepared in step 2 and piece E right sides together. Fuse the fusible fleece or single-sided fusible batting on the wrong side (figure 3).

4 Attach the interfacing to the wrong side of the backing for the basket front piece. Sew the fused backing and the basket front top prepared in step 3 right sides together. Turn right side out, put the template plastic inside, and baste along the bottom edge. Make two pieces (figure 4).

5 Repeat steps 2 through 4 to make two basket side pieces (figure 5).

6 Fuse the fusible fleece or single-sided fusible batting on the wrong side of the basket bottom top. Sew the basket bottom and the basket

front and side pieces together. Press the seam allowances toward the basket bottom. Place the template plastic in the basket bottom below the seam allowances (figure 6).

Dimensional Diagram

Front piece
top (pieced, appliquéd, and embroidered)
fusible batting
backing (yellow print)
interfacing
template plastic

2 pieces each

Side
top (pieced, appliquéd, and embroidered)
fusible batting
backing (yellow print)
interfacing
template plastic

2 pieces each

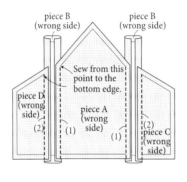

0.05 cm [¹⁄₁₆"]

0.1 cm [¹⁄₁₆"]

template plastic

11 cm [4⅜"]

Appliqué.

piece B

piece B

piece C

Appliqué.

piece D

Appliqué.

0.1 cm [¹⁄₁₆"]

template plastic

6.5 cm [2⅝"]

Outline stitch along outer edges.

piece F

piece A

1 cm [³⁄₈"]

piece E

0.3 cm [⅛"]

14 cm [5½"]

0.3 cm [⅛"]

10 cm [4"]

piece G

Basket bottom
top (dark brown check)
fusible batting
backing (yellow print)
interfacing
template plastic

1 piece each

0.2 cm [¹⁄₁₆"]

template plastic

10 cm [4"]

- Do not add seam allowances when cutting fusible batting, interfacing, and template plastic.
- When cutting appliqués, add 0.3 to 0.4 cm [⅛"] seam allowances. Cut all other pieces with 0.7 cm [¼"] seam allowances.

Figure 1: Sewing together pieces A–D

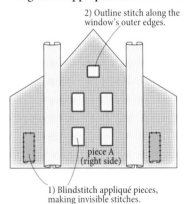

piece B (wrong side)

piece B (wrong side)

Sew from this point to the bottom edge.

piece D (wrong side)

piece A (wrong side)

piece C (wrong side)

(2)   (1)   (1)   (2)

Figure 2: Appliqués and embroideries

2) Outline stitch along the window's outer edges.

piece A (right side)

1) Blindstitch appliqué pieces, making invisible stitches.

Figure 3: Making the front piece top

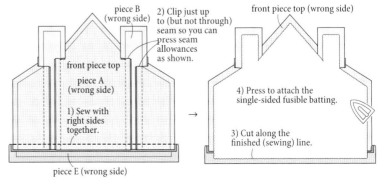

front piece top (wrong side)

piece B (wrong side)

2) Clip just up to (but not through) seam so you can press seam allowances as shown.

front piece top

piece A (wrong side)

1) Sew with right sides together.

piece E (wrong side)

front piece top (wrong side)

4) Press to attach the single-sided fusible batting.

3) Cut along the finished (sewing) line.

7 Fuse the interfacing to the wrong side of the basket bottom backing, fold under the seam allowances, and blindstitch to the basket bottom prepared in step 6 (figure 7).

8 Lift up the front and side pieces prepared in step 7. Use a curved needle to blindstitch each corner (see finished basket diagram).

Figure 4: Sewing front piece top and backing together

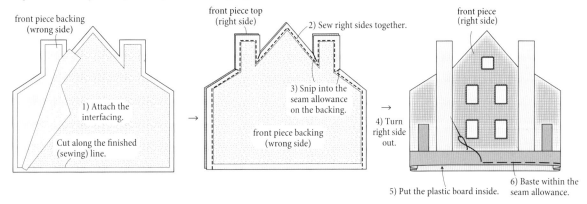

front piece backing (wrong side)

front piece top (right side)

2) Sew right sides together.

1) Attach the interfacing.

Cut along the finished (sewing) line.

3) Snip into the seam allowance on the backing.

front piece backing (wrong side)

4) Turn right side out.

front piece (right side)

5) Put the plastic board inside.

6) Baste within the seam allowance.

Figure 5: Making the side pieces

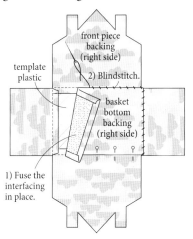

side piece top (right side)

4) Fuse the batting in place.

1) Appliqué.

2) Outline stitch.

3) Sew right sides together.

side piece top (right side)

5) Fuse the interfacing on the backing.

6) Sew right sides together.

side piece backing (wrong side)

7) Turn right side out.

side piece top (right side)

9) Baste within the seam allowance.

8) Put the template plastic inside.

Figure 6: Making the basket bottom top

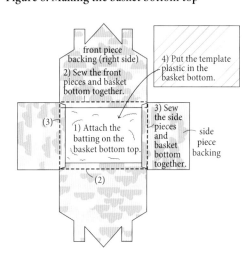

front piece backing (right side)

2) Sew the front pieces and basket bottom together.

4) Put the template plastic in the basket bottom.

(3)

1) Attach the batting on the basket bottom top.

3) Sew the side pieces and basket bottom together.

side piece backing

(2)

Figure 7: Securing the basket bottom backing

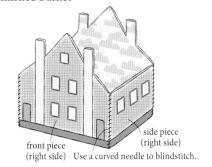

front piece backing (right side)

2) Blindstitch.

template plastic

basket bottom backing (right side)

1) Fuse the interfacing in place.

Finished Basket

front piece (right side)

side piece (right side)

Use a curved needle to blindstitch.

Winter Birds Clasp Purse shown on p. 16

Finished Measurements

- Length (l): approx. 11 cm [4⅜"]; opening width: approx. 12 cm [4¾"]
- The template/pattern can be found on side D of the pattern sheet inserts.

Materials Needed

Cottons
- Gray print - 40 x 15 cm [16" x 6"] (pouch front and back)
- Dark brown check - 18 x 10 cm [8" x 4"] (pouch bottom)
- Gray stripe - 30 x 15 cm [12" x 6"] (gusset)
- Assorted fat quarters or scraps (10 pieces) (appliqués)
- Check - 35 x 30 cm [14" x 12"] (backing)
Batting - 35 x 30 cm [14" x 12"]
Metal clasp purse frame - 12 x 5.5 cm [4¾" x 2⅛"]
Thin paper string or twine - 50 cm [20"]
Embroidery floss: olive, brown, gray, black, aqua

Instructions

1 Referring to the dimensional diagram above right and the full-size template on side D of the pattern sheet inserts, appliqué pieces 1 to 14 in numerical order to the pouch front background fabric. Stitch embroideries. Appliqué and embroider the background fabric for the pouch back.
2 Sew the pouch front and back pieces to the top and bottom edges of the pouch bottom respectively. Press the seam allowances toward the pouch bottom.
3 Draw quilting lines on the pouch top (prepared in step 2) and gusset top.
4 Referring to figure 1, put the pouch top and backing right sides together. Put the batting on the wrong side of the backing. Sew all around except for the opening to turn right side out. Trim off the excess batting. Turn right side out, and blindstitch to close the opening. Quilt.
5 Referring to the dimensional diagram, in the same manner as the pouch, make the gussets and quilt them.
6 With right sides together, match centers of pouch and one gusset. Whipstitch top layers together. Next, ladder stitch to sew the backing layers together (see steps 1 and 2 of figure 2 for visuals of this process). Repeat to sew the remaining gusset to the other end of the case.
7 Turn right side out, and attach the metal clasp purse frame (see figure 2 on p. 69).

Dimensional Diagram

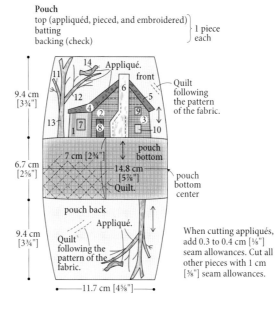

Pouch
top (appliquéd, pieced, and embroidered)
batting
backing (check) } 1 piece each

9.4 cm [3¾"]

14 Appliqué.
11
12 front
6
4 5
13 2 9
1 7 8 3
10

Quilt following the pattern of the fabric.

6.7 cm [2⅝"]
7 cm [2¾"]
14.8 cm [5⅞"] Quilt.
pouch bottom
pouch bottom center

9.4 cm [3¾"]
pouch back
Appliqué.
Quilt following the pattern of the fabric.

11.7 cm [4⅝"]

When cutting appliqués, add 0.3 to 0.4 cm [⅛"] seam allowances. Cut all other pieces with 1 cm [⅜"] seam allowances.

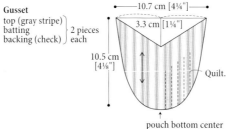

Gusset
top (gray stripe)
batting
backing (check) } 2 pieces each

10.7 cm [4¼"]
3.3 cm [1¼"]
10.5 cm [4⅛"]
Quilt.
pouch bottom center

Figure 2: Sewing the pouch and gusset together

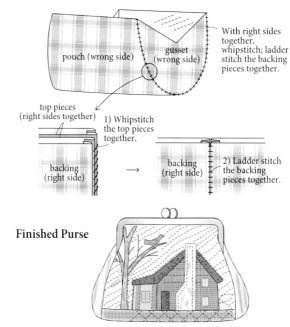

pouch (wrong side)
gusset (wrong side)

With right sides together, whipstitch; ladder stitch the backing pieces together.

top pieces (right sides together)

backing (right side)
1) Whipstitch the top pieces together.

backing (right side)
2) Ladder stitch the backing pieces together.

Finished Purse

Figure 1: Sewing the pouch

backing batting (right side) right sides together

pouch top (wrong side)
front

pouch back

1) Sew 3 layers.

Leave open 5 to 6 cm [2" to 2⅜"].

2) Trim to 0.1 cm [¹⁄₁₆"] from the seam.

batting

Leave open.

3) Turn right side out.

Quilt.

Stitch in the ditch around the appliqués.

5) Quilt.

Quilt following the pattern of the fabric.

4) Blindstitch.

Lunch Bag shown on p. 24

Finished Measurements

- Side length: approx. 11 cm [4⅜"]; bag bottom: approx. 11 x 11 cm [4⅜" x 4⅜"]
- The template/pattern can be found on side D of the pattern sheet inserts.

Materials Needed

Cottons
- Blue check - 35 x 45 cm [14" x 18"] (front piece A, back piece top)
- Blue ombré plaid - 12 x 12 cm [5" x 5"] (front piece B)
- Brown check - 35 x 35 cm [14" x 14"] (side top)
- Assorted fat quarters or scraps (6 pieces) (patchwork pieces 1–7)
- Blue - 60 x 45 cm [24" x 18"] (backing)
Embroidery floss: black, green, blue

Instructions

1 Referring to the dimensional diagram above right and the full-size template on side D of the pattern sheet inserts, trace the design on piece A for the bag front. Next, appliqué pieces 1–7 in numerical order, making invisible stitches. Stitch embroideries.

2 Sew pieces A and B for the bag front right sides together. Press the seam allowance toward piece B.

3 Put the top and backing for the bag front right sides together. Sew all around the edges, leaving an opening for turning. Turn right side out, press flat, and blindstitch to close the opening (figure 1). Sew the bag back in the same manner.

4 Put the top and backing for the bag side right sides together. Sew all around except for the top edge (figure 2). Turn right side out from the top edge and press flat. Make two pieces.

5 Put the front and side pieces right sides together. From the marked point to the bag bottom center, whipstitch to sew the top pieces together. Use a ladder stitch to sew the backing pieces together (see figure 3 below as well as steps 1 and 2 of figure 2 on p. 76). In the same manner, sew together the four bag pieces.

6 Put the top edge of the two side pieces together. Sew along the top edge. Trim three of the seam allowances to roughly 0.7 cm [¼"] from the seam, and use the wide seam allowance to bind the trimmed seam (figure 4).

Dimensional Diagram

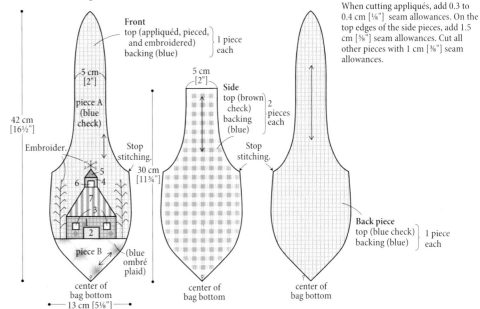

When cutting appliqués, add 0.3 to 0.4 cm [⅛"] seam allowances. On the top edges of the side pieces, add 1.5 cm [⅝"] seam allowances. Cut all other pieces with 1 cm [⅜"] seam allowances.

Figure 1: Sewing the front piece

Figure 2: Sewing the sides

Figure 3: Joining the front and side pieces

Figure 4: Sewing the top edges of the side pieces

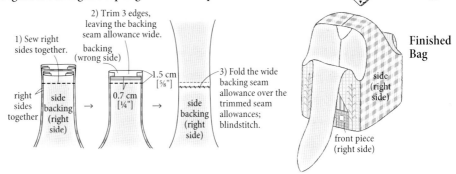

Finished Bag

Shoulder Bag shown on p. 26

front

back

Finished Measurements

- Length (l): 20.7 cm [8⅛"]; width (w): approx. 32 cm [12⅝"]; gusset width: approx. 3.5 cm [1⅜"]
- The template/pattern can be found on side B of the pattern sheet inserts.

Materials Needed

Cottons

- Check A - 10 x 10 cm [4" x 4"] (appliqués)
- Check B - 10 x 10 cm [4" x 4"] (tabs)
- Print C - 75 x 50 cm [30" x 20"] (bag front and back, opening, facing, binding for bag opening)
- Print D - 80 x 60 cm [32" x 24"] (lining, inner pocket, backing, zippered pocket fabric A and B, bias binding for seam allowances)

Lightweight interfacing - 35 x 5 cm [14" x 2"] (facing, tabs)

Zipper - 27 cm [10⅝"] long - 2 pieces

Woven linen tape - 3 x 150 cm [1⅛" x 59"] (shoulder straps A and B)

Corner ring/slide buckle (inside width 3 cm [1⅛"]) - 1 piece each

Instructions

1 Referring to the dimensional diagram above right and the full-size template on side B of the pattern sheet inserts, stitch house appliqués on the bag front top. Then sew the darts; press the seam allowances toward the bag bottom (figure 1).

2 Put the bag back top and zippered pocket fabric A wrong sides together. Baste the seam allowance on the edges. Fuse the lightweight interfacing on the facing. Put the fused facing and bag back top right sides together, and sew around where the zipper will be installed. Slit in the middle and press the facing toward zippered pocket fabric A. Tuck under the seam allowances around the outer edges of the facing, and blindstitch (figure 2).

3 Referring to figure 3, make the tabs.

4 Sew the zipper and tabs to the bag back top. Put zippered pocket fabric B on the wrong side of the bag back top. Baste around the edges (figure 4).

5 Baste shoulder straps A and B at an angle on the right side of the bag front top. Sew the bag back top prepared in step 4 and the bag front top right sides together. Turn right side out (figure 5).

6 Make the inner pocket, and sew it to the bag divider, stitching along the center of the inner pocket (figure 6).

7 Sew the darts on the front lining as done in step 1. Sew the front and back lining together on the side and bottom edges, right sides together. Do not turn right side out. Insert the lining into the bag body prepared in step 5. Baste the lining to the bag body along the top opening.

8 To make the zippered opening, put the opening top and backing right sides together. Sandwich a zipper in between, and sew along the edge (figure 7). Repeat on the other side of the zipper. Sew the angled edges of the bag opening together as shown.

9 Put the bag opening at the top edge of the bag, wrong sides together. Use the 3.5 cm [1⅜"] bias strip to bind the opening (figure 8).

10 Make the shoulder strap (figure 9).

Dimensional Diagram

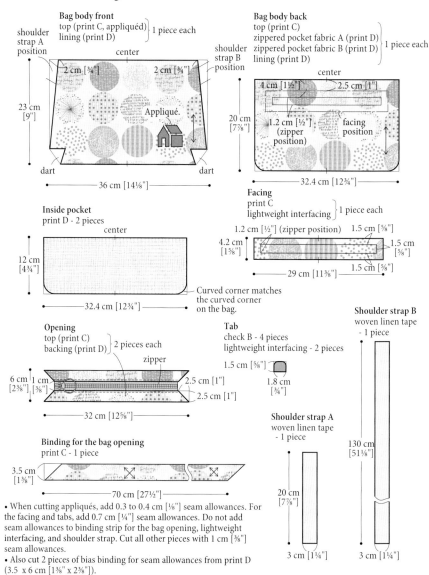

- When cutting appliqués, add 0.3 to 0.4 cm [⅛"] seam allowances. For the facing and tabs, add 0.7 cm [¼"] seam allowances. Do not add seam allowances to binding strip for the bag opening, lightweight interfacing, and shoulder strap. Cut all other pieces with 1 cm [⅜"] seam allowances.
- Also cut 2 pieces of bias binding for seam allowances from print D (3.5 x 6 cm [1⅜" x 2⅜"]).

How to put the bag front and back pieces together

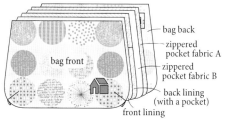

Figure 1: Sewing darts

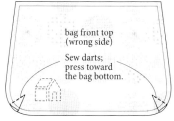

Figure 2: Sewing the facing

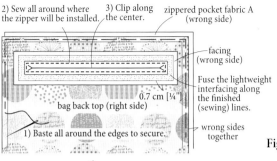

2) Sew all around where the zipper will be installed.

3) Clip along the center.

zippered pocket fabric A (wrong side)

facing (wrong side)

Fuse the lightweight interfacing along the finished (sewing) lines.

0.7 cm [¼"]

bag back top (right side)

1) Baste all around the edges to secure.

wrong sides together

bag back top (wrong side)

facing (right side)

4) Turn the facing right side out. Turn under the seam allowances and blindstitch with invisible stitches to the backing.

zipper position

zippered pocket fabric A (right side)

Figure 3: Making tabs

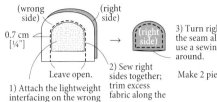

(wrong side)   (right side)

0.7 cm [¼"]

Leave open.

1) Attach the lightweight interfacing on the wrong side of 1 tab piece.

2) Sew right sides together; trim excess fabric along the seam.

(right side)

3) Turn right side out; tuck under the seam allowance on the opening; use a sewing machine to topstitch all around.

Make 2 pieces.

Figure 5: Attaching shoulder straps A and B and sewing bag pieces together

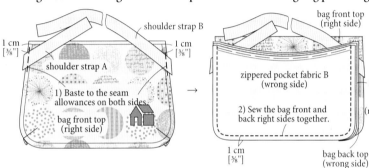

shoulder strap B

bag front top (right side)

1 cm [⅜"]

1 cm [⅜"]

shoulder strap A

1) Baste to the seam allowances on both sides.

bag front top (right side)

zippered pocket fabric B (wrong side)

zippered pocket fabric A (right side)

2) Sew the bag front and back right sides together.

1 cm [⅜"]

bag back top (wrong side)

Figure 4: Sewing the zipper and tabs

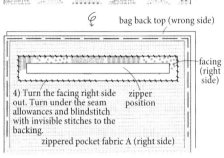

zippered pocket fabric A (wrong side)

4) Put the zippered pocket fabric A and B together; baste.

zippered pocket fabric B (right side)

bag back top (right side)

zipper (wrong side)

Tuck under both edges.

2) Blindstitch zipper tape in place.

1) Put the zipper on the right side of the zippered pocket fabric A; adjust the location of the zipper; topstitch with a sewing machine.

3) Machine sew to attach tabs to right and left sides of the zipper.

Figure 6: Making and attaching the inner pocket

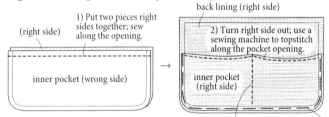

1) Put two pieces right sides together; sew along the opening.

(right side)

back lining (right side)

2) Turn right side out; use a sewing machine to topstitch along the pocket opening.

inner pocket (wrong side)

inner pocket (right side)

3) Put the inner pocket on the bag divider; sew along the central dividing line.

4) Baste on the seam allowance.

Figure 7: Making the bag opening

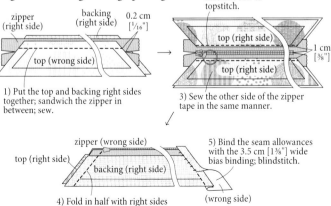

zipper (right side)

backing (right side)

0.2 cm [¹⁄₁₆"]

top (wrong side)

1) Put the top and backing right sides together; sandwich the zipper in between; sew.

2) Turn right side out; machine sew to topstitch.

top (right side)

top (right side)

1 cm [⅜"]

3) Sew the other side of the zipper tape in the same manner.

zipper (wrong side)

top (right side)

backing (right side)

(wrong side)

5) Bind the seam allowances with the 3.5 cm [1⅜"] wide bias binding; blindstitch.

4) Fold in half with right sides together; sew along both sides.

Figure 8: Sewing the bag and opening together

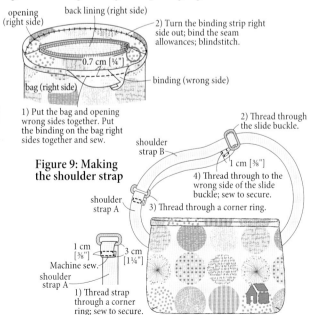

opening (right side)

back lining (right side)

2) Turn the binding strip right side out; bind the seam allowances; blindstitch.

0.7 cm [¼"]

bag (right side)

binding (wrong side)

1) Put the bag and opening wrong sides together. Put the binding on the bag right sides together and sew.

Figure 9: Making the shoulder strap

2) Thread through the slide buckle.

shoulder strap B

1 cm [⅜"]

4) Thread through to the wrong side of the slide buckle; sew to secure.

shoulder strap A

3) Thread through a corner ring.

1 cm [⅜"]

3 cm [1¼"]

Machine sew.

shoulder strap A

1) Thread strap through a corner ring; sew to secure.

Bottle Carrier

shown on p. 28

Finished Measurements

- Length (l): 30 cm [11¾"]; opening width: 18 cm [7"]; bag bottom gusset: 10 x 8 cm [3⅞" x 3⅛"]
- The template/pattern can be found on side A of the pattern sheet inserts.

Materials Needed

Cottons
- Blue ombré plaid - 40 x 25 cm [16" x 10"] (background fabric)
- Navy blue check - 40 x 10 cm [16" x 4"] (bag bottom)
- Assorted fat quarters or scraps in brown (approx. 10 pieces) (pieces A and B)
- Gray check, blue, navy blue print, navy blue woven homespun, beige print, gray print (appliqués)
- Black woven homespun - 40 x 5 cm [16" x 2"] (bag opening)
- Beige check - 40 x 40 cm [16" x 16"] (backing)
Woven cotton webbing (black) - 3 x 42 cm [1⅛" x 16½"] (handle)

Embroidery floss: navy blue, gray

Instructions

1 Referring to the dimensional diagram above right and the full-size template on side A of the pattern sheet inserts, blindstitch appliqué pieces onto the background fabric, making invisible stitches. Stitch embroideries.

2 Piece A and B rectangles and squares together to make the "roof" for the bag.

3 Referring to the dimensional diagram, sew together the bag opening, the patchwork from step 2, the appliquéd fabric from step 1, and the bag bottom.

4 Fold the top (prepared in step 3) right sides together, and sew along the side and bottom edges. Sew along the raw edges at the bag bottom to make a gusset; press the seams open (figure 1).

5 In the same manner as the top, sew along the side edges of the backing, but leave 7 to 8 cm [2¾" to 3¼"] open to turn right side out. Sew the bag bottom and gusset as in step 4.

6 Baste the woven cotton webbing at the top edge of the bag top. Put the backing and the top right sides together, and sew along the top edge (figure 2).

7 Turn right side out from the opening on the backing, smooth out the wrinkles, and blindstitch to close the opening. Topstitch along the top edge of the bag opening.

Dimensional Diagram

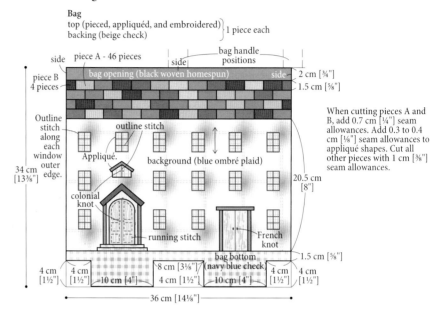

When cutting pieces A and B, add 0.7 cm [¼"] seam allowances. Add 0.3 to 0.4 cm [⅛"] seam allowances to appliqué shapes. Cut all other pieces with 1 cm [⅜"] seam allowances.

Figure 1: Sewing the sides, bag bottom, and gusset

Figure 2: Sewing the top edges

Finished Carrier

Zippered Sewing Case shown on p. 30

Finished Measurements

- Length (l): 14 cm [5½"]; width (w): 23 cm [9"]; height (h): 7.7 cm [3"]
- The lid template/pattern can be found on side B of the pattern sheet inserts.

Materials Needed

Cottons
- Assorted fat quarters or scraps (approx. 20 pieces) (appliqués)
- Blue-gray print - 27 x 18 cm [11" x 8"] (lid background fabric)
- Brown print - 80 x 15 cm [32" x 6"] (gusset)
- Brown polka dot - 27 x 18 cm [11" x 8"] (case bottom)
- Black woven homespun - 10 x 15 cm [4" x 6"] (tabs)
- Gray print - 110 x 50 cm [44" x 20"] (lid lining; backing for lid, gussets, and case bottom; binding)

Thin cotton - 80 x 50 cm [32" x 20"] (facing)
Thick tulle - 25 x 15 cm [10" x 6"] (lid lining)
Batting - 110 x 50 cm [44" x 20"]
Heavyweight interfacing - 75 x 50 cm [30" x 20"]
Double-sided fusible web
Zippers
- 60 cm [23⅝"] long (with double sliders; for gusset. If you can't find a zipper like this, you can use 2 shorter zippers and have them meet in the middle of the gusset.)
- 20 cm [7⅞"] long (lid lining)

Embroidery floss: dark brown, cream, red, blue, blue gray, brown, beige, yellow-green, medium brown

Instructions

1 Referring to the dimensional diagram above right and the full-size template on side B of the pattern sheet inserts, trace the design on the lid background fabric. Blindstitch appliqué pieces 1 to 30 in numerical order to the lid background fabric (see the numbers on the full-size template), making invisible stitches. Stitch embroideries, and draw quilting motifs.

2 Make a quilt sandwich with the lid facing, batting, and the lid top prepared in step 1. Baste and quilt.

3 Quilt the case bottom top (figure 1).

(Turn to page 83 for remaining instructions.)

Dimensional Diagram

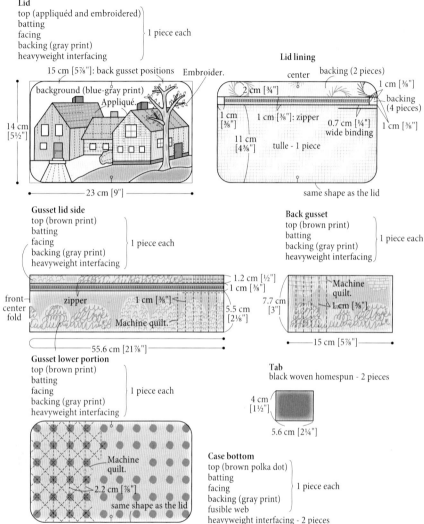

- When cutting out appliqués, add 0.3 to 0.4 cm [⅛"] seam allowances. For the case lid and bottom batting and facing, add 2 cm [¾"] seam allowances. Do not add any seam allowance to the heavyweight interfacing or fusible web. Cut all other pieces with 1 cm [⅜"] seam allowances.
- To make the piping (gray print) for the inner pocket on the lid lining, cut a 2.5 cm [1"] wide bias fabric strip 25 cm [9¾"] long.

Figure 1: Quilting the case bottom top

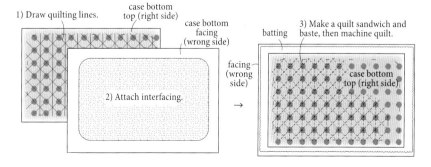

1) Draw quilting lines.
2) Attach interfacing.
3) Make a quilt sandwich and baste, then machine quilt.

Figure 2: Inserting a zipper into the gusset

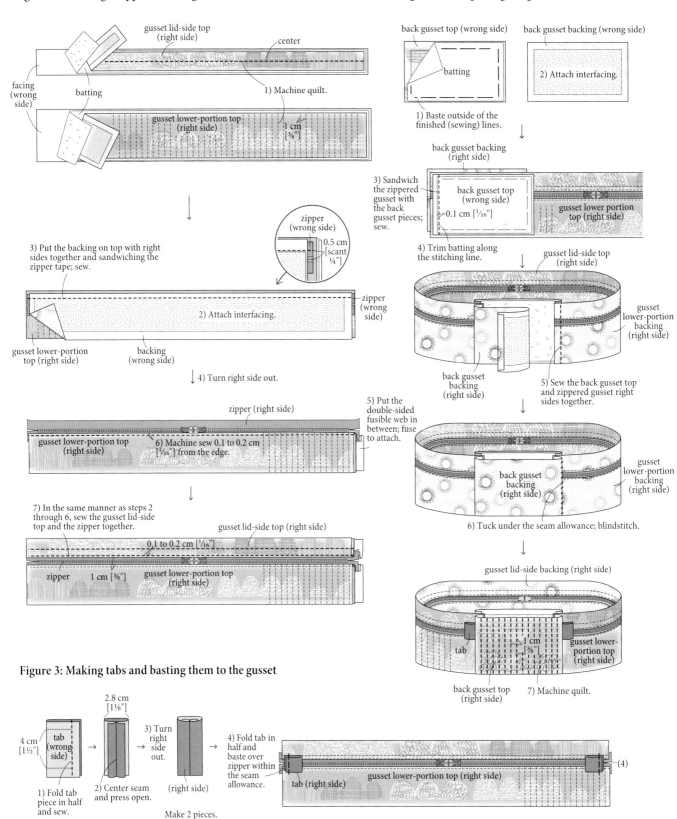

gusset lid-side top (right side)

center

facing (wrong side)

batting

1) Machine quilt.

gusset lower-portion top (right side)

1 cm [⅜"]

3) Put the backing on top with right sides together and sandwiching the zipper tape; sew.

zipper (wrong side)

0.5 cm [scant ¼"]

2) Attach interfacing.

zipper (wrong side)

gusset lower-portion top (right side)

backing (wrong side)

4) Turn right side out.

zipper (right side)

gusset lower-portion top (right side)

6) Machine sew 0.1 to 0.2 cm [¹⁄₁₆"] from the edge.

5) Put the double-sided fusible web in between; fuse to attach.

7) In the same manner as steps 2 through 6, sew the gusset lid-side top and the zipper together.

gusset lid-side top (right side)

0.1 to 0.2 cm [¹⁄₁₆"]

zipper

1 cm [⅜"]

gusset lower-portion top (right side)

Figure 3: Making tabs and basting them to the gusset

4 cm [1½"]

tab (wrong side)

1) Fold tab piece in half and sew.

2.8 cm [1⅛"]

2) Center seam and press open.

3) Turn right side out.

(right side)

Make 2 pieces.

4) Fold tab in half and baste over zipper within the seam allowance.

tab (right side)

gusset lower-portion top (right side)

(4)

Figure 4: Completing the gusset

back gusset top (wrong side)

batting

1) Baste outside of the finished (sewing) lines.

back gusset backing (wrong side)

2) Attach interfacing.

back gusset backing (right side)

3) Sandwich the zippered gusset with the back gusset pieces; sew.

back gusset top (wrong side)

0.1 cm [¹⁄₁₆"]

gusset lower portion top (right side)

4) Trim batting along the stitching line.

gusset lid-side top (right side)

gusset lower-portion backing (right side)

back gusset backing (right side)

5) Sew the back gusset top and zippered gusset right sides together.

back gusset backing (right side)

gusset lower-portion backing (right side)

6) Tuck under the seam allowance; blindstitch.

gusset lid-side backing (right side)

tab

1 cm [⅜"]

gusset lower-portion top (right side)

back gusset top (right side)

7) Machine quilt.

82

(continued from page 81)

4 Insert the zipper into the gusset (figure 2).
5 Make tabs and baste them to the gusset (figure 3).
6 Sew the zippered gusset and back gusset together (figure 4).
7 Sew the gusset and quilted case bottom top

together. In the same manner, sew the gusset and the lid prepared in steps 1 and 2 together (figure 5).
8 Make the case bottom backing. First, turn the piece prepared in step 7 right side out and smooth out the winkles. Measure the inner dimensions of the pouch bottom to adjust the

size of the case bottom backing. Fuse interfacing on the wrong side and sew running stitches along four corners to gather (figure 6).
9 Make the lid lining (figure 7).
10 Blindstitch the lid lining and case bottom backing together (figure 8).

Figure 5: Sewing the gusset, case bottom top, and lid top together

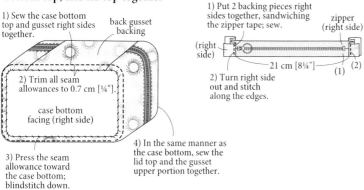

1) Sew the case bottom top and gusset right sides together.

back gusset backing

2) Trim all seam allowances to 0.7 cm [¼"].

case bottom facing (right side)

3) Press the seam allowance toward the case bottom; blindstitch down.

4) In the same manner as the case bottom, sew the lid top and the gusset upper portion together.

Figure 7: Making the lid lining

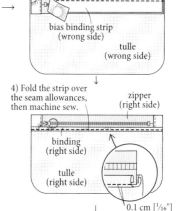

1) Put 2 backing pieces right sides together, sandwiching the zipper tape; sew.

zipper (right side)

(right side)

21 cm [8¼"]

(1)   (2)

2) Turn right side out and stitch along the edges.

zipper (right side)

3) Sew.

0.7 cm [¼"]

bias binding strip (wrong side)

tulle (wrong side)

4) Fold the strip over the seam allowances, then machine sew.

zipper (right side)

binding (right side)

tulle (right side)

0.1 cm [¹⁄₁₆"]

5) Put 2 backing pieces right sides together, sandwiching the zipper tape; sew. Turn right side out and topstitch twice.

backing (right side)

(wrong side)

0.7 cm [¼"]

tulle (right side)

6) Put the tulle on the lid backing; use running stitch on the seam allowance.

lid lining (right side) (tulle; right side)

lid backing (Fuse the interfacing to the wrong side.)

7) Press to fold over the seam allowances; topstitch from the right side.

0.1 cm [¹⁄₁₆"]

lid lining (wrong side)

Figure 6: Making the case bottom backing

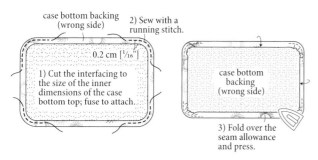

case bottom backing (wrong side)

2) Sew with a running stitch.

0.2 cm [¹⁄₁₆"]

1) Cut the interfacing to the size of the inner dimensions of the case bottom top; fuse to attach.

case bottom backing (wrong side)

3) Fold over the seam allowance and press.

Figure 8: Securing the lid lining and bottom backing

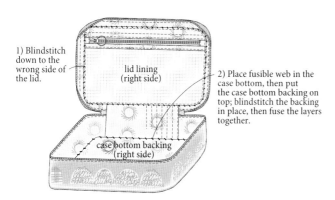

1) Blindstitch down to the wrong side of the lid.

lid lining (right side)

2) Place fusible web in the case bottom, then put the case bottom backing on top; blindstitch the backing in place, then fuse the layers together.

case bottom backing (right side)

Market Bag shown on p. 34

Finished Measurements

- Length (l): approx. 34 cm [13⅜"]; width (w): 18 cm [7"]; bag side gusset width: 7 cm [2¾"]
- The template/pattern can be found on side D of the pattern sheet inserts.

Materials Needed

Cottons
- Green print - 45 x 60 cm [18" x 24"] (top of bag front and back)
- Gray print - 45 x 60 cm [18" x 24"] (backing)
- Brown print - 10 x 15 cm [4" x 6"] (pieces 1 and 11)
- Beige woven homespun - 12 x 7 cm [5" x 3"] (piece 2)
- Red polka dot - 15 x 15 cm [6" x 6"] (piece 3)
- Gray print - 6 x 7 cm [2½" x 3"] (piece 4)
- Scraps of blue print, yellow check, solid red, dark brown check, black, dark brown print, and beige (pieces 5 to 10, and 12)
- Moss green - 60 x 50 cm [24" x 20"] (binding)
Embroidery floss: dark brown, blue, black, yellow, ecru, brown

Instructions

1 Referring to the dimensional diagram above right and the full-size template on side D of the pattern sheet inserts, trace the design onto the bag front top (background fabric). Blindstitch pieces 1 to 12 in numerical order to the bag front top, making invisible stitches. Stitch embroideries.

2 Put the bag front top (prepared in step 1) and bag back top right sides together, and sew along both sides (figure 1). Press the seams open.

3 Put the bag front handles together. Sew along the top edge. Repeat with the bag back handles (figure 2). Press the seams open, turn right side out, and smooth out the wrinkles.

4 In the same manner as steps 2 and 3, sew the backing, stitching along the sides and top edge of the bag handles.

5 Put the bag front/back backing (prepared in step 4) inside the bag front/back top, wrong sides together. Baste to secure around the bag handles and bottom.

6 Use the 2.5 cm [1"] wide bias strips to bind the bag handles (figure 3).

7 Fold both sides of the bag toward the inside 3.5 cm [1⅜"] from the edge to make a pleat.

Use the remaining 2.5 cm [1"] wide bias strip to bind the bag bottom (refer to the "Finished Bag" illustration).

8 Fold the bag handles in half lengthwise, and sew to secure approximately 6 cm [2⅜"] at the center (refer to the "Finished Bag" illustration).

Dimensional Diagram

Bag
front top (appliquéd and embroidered) 1 piece each
bag back top (green print)
backing (gray print) - 2 pieces

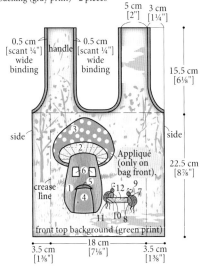

5 cm [2"]   3 cm [1¼"]

0.5 cm [scant ¼"] wide binding   handle   0.5 cm [scant ¼"] wide binding

15.5 cm [6⅛"]

22.5 cm [8⅞"]

side   side

Appliqué (only on bag front)

crease line

front top background (green print)

3.5 cm [1⅜"]   18 cm [7⅛"]   3.5 cm [1⅜"]

- For the binding, cut moss green fabric on the bias to make 2.5 cm [1"] wide bias strips. Cut 2 pieces 42 cm [17"] long, 1 piece 72 cm [29"] long, and 1 piece 22 cm [9"] long.
- When cutting appliqués, add 0.3 to 0.4 cm [⅛"] seam allowances. On both sides of the bag and handles, add 1 cm [⅜"] seam allowances. Cut all other pieces with 0.5 cm [scant ¼"] seam allowances.
- Appliqué pieces 1 to 12 in numerical order.
- See the full-size template for the embroidery designs.

Figure 1: Sewing sides

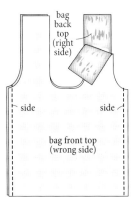

bag back top (right side)

side   side

bag front top (wrong side)

Figure 2: Sewing handle top edges

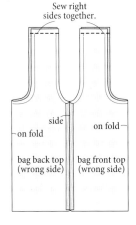

Sew right sides together.

side
on fold   on fold

bag back top (wrong side)   bag front top (wrong side)

Figure 3: Binding

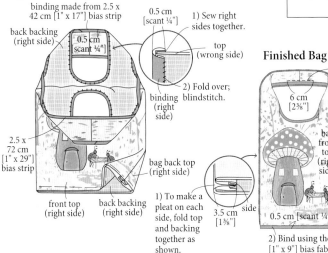

binding made from 2.5 x 42 cm [1" x 17"] bias strip

back backing (right side)

0.5 cm [scant ¼"]

0.5 cm [scant ¼"]

1) Sew right sides together.

top (wrong side)

2) Fold over; binding blindstitch. (right side)

2.5 x 72 cm [1" x 29"] bias strip

front top (right side)   back backing (right side)

bag back top (right side)

1) To make a pleat on each side, fold top and backing together as shown.

Finished Bag

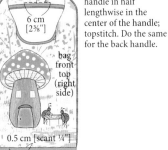

3) Fold the front handle in half lengthwise in the center of the handle; topstitch. Do the same for the back handle.

6 cm [2⅜"]

bag front top (right side)

3.5 cm [1⅜"]   side

0.5 cm [scant ¼"]

2) Bind using the 2.5 x 22 cm [1" x 9"] bias fabric.

Everyday Handbag *shown on p. 38*

Finished Measurements

- Length (l): 23.7 cm [9⅜"]; width (w): 32 cm [12⅝"]; gusset width: 9 cm [3½"]
- The template/pattern can be found on side B of the pattern sheet inserts.

Materials Needed

Cottons
- Assorted fat quarters or scraps (approx. 30 pieces) (patchwork and appliqués)
- Print A - 10 x 5 cm [4" x 2"] (fabric to bind zipper tape end)
- Check B - 2.5 x 20 cm [1" x 8"] - 2 pieces (patchwork, bias binding for gusset opening)
- Polka-dot woven homespun - 90 x 45 cm [36" x 18"] (bag front and back, gusset, outer pocket, outer pocket backing)
- Stripe - 25 x 20 cm [10" x 8"] (awnings)
- Check C - 10 x 25 cm [4" x 10"] (handles)
- Check D - 35 x 40 cm [14" x 16"] (facing, opening)
- Print E - 15 x 40 cm [6" x 16"] (patchwork, bag bottom)
- Print F - 110 x 55 cm [44" x 22"] (backing, bias binding for seam allowances)
Batting - 90 x 75 cm [36" x 30"]

Low-loft batting - 30 x 15 cm [12" x 6"]
Heavyweight interfacing - 35 x 10 cm [14" x 4"] (bag bottom)
Lightweight interfacing - 40 x 15 cm [16" x 6"] (awnings, facing, handles)
Double-sided fusible web - 35 x 25 cm [14" x 10"] (facing, bag bottom)
Zipper - 40 cm [15¾"] long
Woven linen tape - 3 x 50 cm [1⅛" x 15⅝"] (handles)
Faux leather cord - 0.2 cm [1/16"] in thickness (zipper pull)
1.5 cm [⅝"] metal cube charm to embellish zipper pull
Embroidery floss: black, brown, orange, green, dark gray, gray

Instructions

1 Referring to the dimensional diagrams below and on page 86, and the full-size template on side B of the pattern sheet inserts, piece patches together, and stitch appliqués and embroideries to make the top for the bag front and back. Make a quilt sandwich with each of the top, batting, and backing pieces. Baste and quilt.

2 For the gusset, make a quilt sandwich with the top, batting, and backing. Baste and machine quilt. Draw the finished (sewing) line on the opening edge of the backing. Bind the opening with the bias strip, and blindstitch down to the right side of the backing (figure 1). Make 2.

3 Stitch appliqués and embroideries on the outer pocket top. Layer with batting and backing, and quilt. Baste it to the gusset (figure 2, steps 1 to 5). Make 2.

4 Fuse heavyweight interfacing on the wrong side of the bag bottom backing, and layer with the batting and top. Baste and machine quilt (figure 2, step 6).

5 Put the gusset and bag bottom right sides together with the outer pocket in between. Sew along the bag bottom side, stitching between the marked points. Use the gusset backing to bind the seam allowances (figure 2, steps 7 to 9).

6 Sew the bag front, bag back, and gusset prepared in step 5 right sides together. First sew along both sides, and then sew along the bag bottom, stitching between the marked points. Use the 2.5 cm [1"] wide bias strip to bind the seam allowances. Blindstitch down to the backing side of the bag top (figure 3).

7 Make the handles and baste them onto the bag (figure 4).

8 Make the facing according to the size of the roof portion of the bag. Put the facing and bag right sides together. Sew between the marked points along the opening, and turn right side out (figure 5).

9 Make the opening (figure 6).

10 Put the opening on the inside of the bag, wrong sides together, and baste. Machine sew around the edges from the right side (figure 7, step 1).

11 Insert the double-sided fusible web between the bag and facing, blindstitch the facing, and press to fuse (figure 7, steps 2 and 3).

12 Make the awnings and sew them to the gusset (figure 8).

13 Fold the faux leather cord in half and make a lark's head knot to attach it to the zipper pull. Feed one end of the cord through the metal cube charm and tie a knot with the remaining cord end as shown (refer to the "Finished Bag" illustration). Bind with a tiny strip of fabric to hide the knot.

Dimensional Diagram (Continued on p. 86)

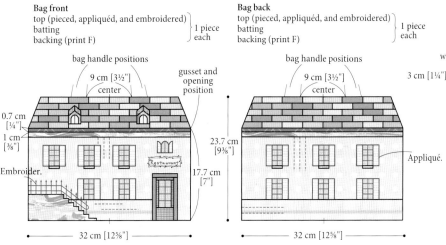

Bag front
top (pieced, appliquéd, and embroidered)
batting
backing (print F) } 1 piece each

bag handle positions
9 cm [3½"] center
gusset and opening position
0.7 cm [¼"]
1 cm [⅜"]
Embroider.
23.7 cm [9⅜"]
17.7 cm [7"]
32 cm [12⅝"]

Bag back
top (pieced, appliquéd, and embroidered)
batting
backing (print F) } 1 piece each

bag handle positions
9 cm [3½"] center
Appliqué.
32 cm [12⅝"]

Bag handles
woven linen tape
check C
lightweight interfacing } 2 pieces each

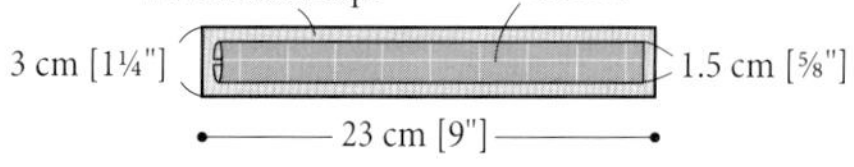

woven linen tape   check C
3 cm [1¼"]   1.5 cm [⅝"]
23 cm [9"]

- When cutting the appliqués (except for the opening and awnings), add 0.3 to 0.4 cm [⅛"] seam allowances. For the bag bottom, gusset, and outer pocket, add 1 cm [⅜"] seam allowances. Cut the backing and batting with 3 cm [1¼"] seam allowances.
- Do not add seam allowances for bias binding for the gusset, individual interfacing pieces, and double-sided fusible web. Cut all other fabric pieces with 0.7 cm [¼"] seam allowances.
- For bias binding for binding the seam allowances, cut 2 bias 2.3 x 73 cm [⅞" x 28¾"] strips from print F (see p. 68 for joining bias strips).

Dimensional Diagram (Continued from p. 85)

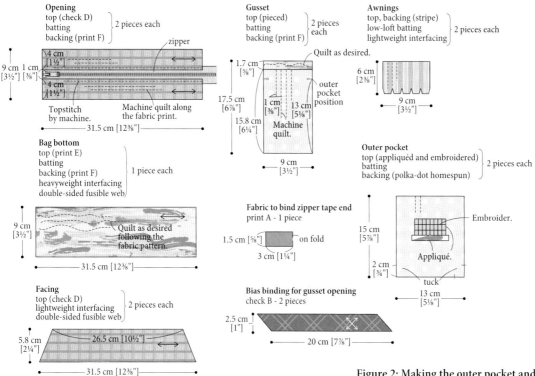

Opening
top (check D)
batting
backing (print F) } 2 pieces each

zipper

9 cm [3½"] 1 cm [⅜"]

4 cm [1½"]

4 cm [1½"]

Topstitch by machine.

Machine quilt along the fabric print.

31.5 cm [12⅜"]

Gusset
top (pieced)
batting
backing (print F) } 2 pieces each

Quilt as desired.

1.7 cm [⅝"]

outer pocket position

1 cm [⅜"] 13 cm [5⅛"]

17.5 cm [6⅞"]

15.8 cm [6¼"]

Machine quilt.

9 cm [3½"]

Awnings
top, backing (stripe)
low-loft batting
lightweight interfacing } 2 pieces each

6 cm [2⅜"]

9 cm [3½"]

Outer pocket
top (appliquéd and embroidered)
batting
backing (polka-dot homespun) } 2 pieces each

Embroider.

15 cm [5⅞"]

Appliqué.

2 cm [¾"]

tuck

13 cm [5⅛"]

Bag bottom
top (print E)
batting
backing (print F)
heavyweight interfacing
double-sided fusible web } 1 piece each

9 cm [3½"]

Quilt as desired following the fabric pattern.

31.5 cm [12⅜"]

Fabric to bind zipper tape end
print A - 1 piece

1.5 cm [⅝"]   on fold

3 cm [1¼"]

Facing
top (check D)
lightweight interfacing
double-sided fusible web } 2 pieces each

5.8 cm [2¼"]

26.5 cm [10½"]

31.5 cm [12⅜"]

Bias binding for gusset opening
check B - 2 pieces

2.5 cm [1"]

20 cm [7⅞"]

Figure 1: Making the gusset

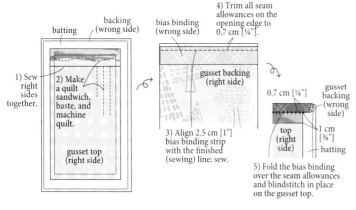

batting

backing (wrong side)

bias binding (wrong side)

4) Trim all seam allowances on the opening edge to 0.7 cm [¼"].

gusset backing (right side)

0.7 cm [¼"]

gusset backing (wrong side)

1) Sew right sides together.

2) Make a quilt sandwich, baste, and machine quilt.

gusset top (right side)

3) Align 2.5 cm [1"] bias binding strip with the finished (sewing) line; sew.

top (right side)

1 cm [⅜"]

batting

5) Fold the bias binding over the seam allowances and blindstitch in place on the gusset top.

Figure 2: Making the outer pocket and bag bottom and sewing them to the gusset

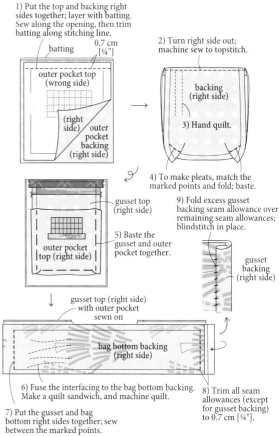

1) Put the top and backing right sides together; layer with batting. Sew along the opening, then trim batting along stitching line.

batting

0.7 cm [¼"]

outer pocket top (wrong side)

(right side) / outer pocket backing (right side)

2) Turn right side out; machine sew to topstitch.

backing (right side)

3) Hand quilt.

4) To make pleats, match the marked points and fold; baste.

gusset top (right side)

outer pocket top (right side)

5) Baste the gusset and outer pocket together.

9) Fold excess gusset backing seam allowance over remaining seam allowances; blindstitch in place.

gusset backing (right side)

gusset top (right side) with outer pocket sewn on

bag bottom backing (right side)

6) Fuse the interfacing to the bag bottom backing. Make a quilt sandwich, and machine quilt.

7) Put the gusset and bag bottom right sides together; sew between the marked points.

8) Trim all seam allowances (except for gusset backing) to 0.7 cm [¼"].

Figure 3: Sewing the bag and gusset, and binding seam allowances

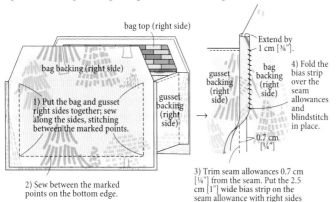

bag top (right side)

bag backing (right side)

1) Put the bag and gusset right sides together; sew along the sides, stitching between the marked points.

gusset backing (right side)

gusset backing (right side)

2) Sew between the marked points on the bottom edge.

Extend by 1 cm [⅜"].

gusset backing (right side)

bag backing (right side)

4) Fold the bias strip over the seam allowances and blindstitch in place.

0.7 cm [¼"]

3) Trim seam allowances 0.7 cm [¼"] from the seam. Put the 2.5 cm [1"] wide bias strip on the seam allowance with right sides together; sew along the edge.

Figure 4: Making and attaching bag handles

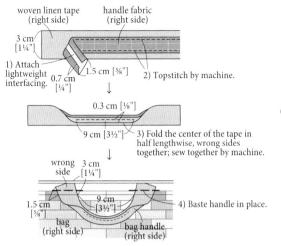

woven linen tape (right side)
handle fabric (right side)

3 cm [1¼"]

1) Attach lightweight interfacing.

0.7 cm [¼"]

1.5 cm [⅝"]

2) Topstitch by machine.

0.3 cm [⅛"]

9 cm [3½"]

3) Fold the center of the tape in half lengthwise, wrong sides together; sew together by machine.

wrong side

3 cm [1¼"]

1.5 cm [⅝"]

9 cm [3½"]

4) Baste handle in place.

bag (right side)

bag handle (right side)

Figure 5: Sewing facing to the bag opening

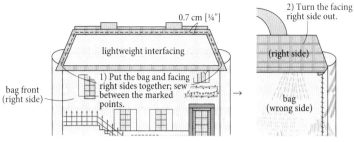

0.7 cm [¼"]

lightweight interfacing

1) Put the bag and facing right sides together; sew between the marked points.

bag front (right side)

2) Turn the facing right side out.

(right side)

bag (wrong side)

In the same manner, sew the facing to the bag back.

Figure 6: Making the bag opening

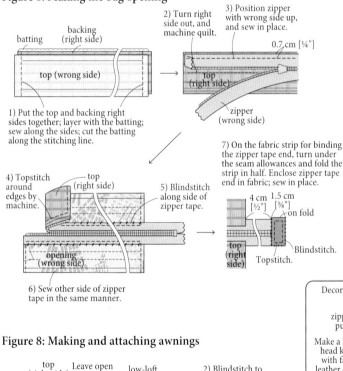

batting
backing (right side)

top (wrong side)

1) Put the top and backing right sides together; layer with the batting; sew along the sides; cut the batting along the stitching line.

2) Turn right side out, and machine quilt.

3) Position zipper with wrong side up, and sew in place.

0.7 cm [¼"]

top (right side)

zipper (wrong side)

4) Topstitch around edges by machine.

top (right side)

5) Blindstitch along side of zipper tape.

opening (wrong side)

6) Sew other side of zipper tape in the same manner.

7) On the fabric strip for binding the zipper tape end, turn under the seam allowances and fold the strip in half. Enclose zipper tape end in fabric; sew in place.

4 cm [½"]

1.5 cm [⅝"]

on fold

top (right side)

Topstitch.

Blindstitch.

Figure 7: Sewing the opening

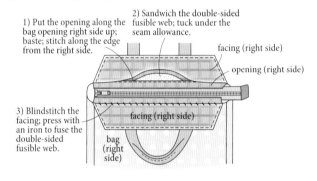

1) Put the opening along the bag opening right side up; baste; stitch along the edge from the right side.

2) Sandwich the double-sided fusible web; tuck under the seam allowance.

facing (right side)

opening (right side)

3) Blindstitch the facing; press with an iron to fuse the double-sided fusible web.

facing (right side)

bag (right side)

Figure 8: Making and attaching awnings

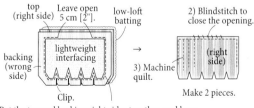

top (right side)
Leave open 5 cm [2"].
low-loft batting

lightweight interfacing

backing (wrong side)

Clip.

2) Blindstitch to close the opening.

3) Machine quilt.

(right side)

Make 2 pieces.

1) Put the top and backing right sides together, and layer with low-loft batting. Sew all around, leaving a 5 cm [2"] opening to turn right side out. Trim batting close to the seam, clip seam allowances, and turn right side out.

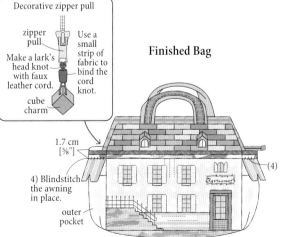

Decorative zipper pull

zipper pull

Use a small strip of fabric to bind the cord knot.

Make a lark's head knot with faux leather cord.

cube charm

Finished Bag

1.7 cm [⅝"]

4) Blindstitch the awning in place.

(4)

outer pocket

Pass Cases shown on p. 40

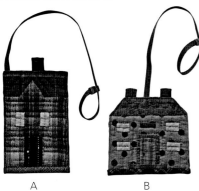

A   B

Making Pass Case A

1 Referring to the dimensional diagram below and the full-size template on side C of the pattern sheet inserts, stitch appliqués and embroideries on the case front (figure 1).
2 Make the chimney, and baste it to the case front (figure 2).
3 Put the appliquéd case top and backing right sides together. Put the batting on the wrong side of the backing. Sew along the sides and top edge. Trim off the excess batting. Turn right side out and quilt (figure 3).

4 Put the upper portion of the case back top and backing right sides together. Put the batting on the wrong side of the backing. Sew, turn right side out, and machine quilt. Repeat with the lower portion of the case back top. Be sure to sandwich the strap between the layers for the upper portion before sewing (figures 4 and 5).
5 Overlap the upper and lower portions of the case back by 0.5 cm [scant ¼"]. Baste the overlapped area together. Put the case front and back wrong sides together. Ladder stitch along all sides, except for the bottom edge, making big stitches. Topstitch by machine (figure 6).

Finished Measurements (not including chimneys)

- A: length (l): 11.7 cm [4⅝"]; width (w): 8 cm [3⅛"]
- B: length (l): 10.2 cm [4"]; width (w): 11 cm [4⅜"]
- The template/pattern can be found on side C of the pattern sheet inserts.

Materials Needed for A

Cottons
- Blue plaid - 50 x 15 cm [20" x 6"] (case front, case back lower portion, backing, strap)
- Red plaid - 20 x 10 cm [8" x 4"] (case back upper portion, roof)
- Dark brown check - 8 x 4 cm [4" x 2"] (chimney)
- Assorted fat quarters or scraps (2 pieces) (appliqués)
- Green check - 15 x 10 cm [6" x 4"] (binding)
Low-loft batting - 25 x 20 cm [10" x 8"]
Strap - 0.6 x 35 cm [¼" x 13¾"]
Embroidery floss: gray

Materials Needed for B

Cottons
- Cream polka dot - 60 x 15 cm [24" x 6"] (case front, case back lower portion, backing)
- Blue print - 30 x 10 cm [12" x 4"] (case back upper portion, appliqués, backing)
- Brown print - 10 x 10 cm [4" x 4"] (chimneys)
- Assorted fat quarters or scraps (5 pieces) (appliqués, strap)
- Black plaid - 15 x 10 cm [6" x 4"] (binding)
Low-loft batting - 30 x 20 cm [12" x 8"]
Strap - 0.8 x 35 cm [⅜" x 13¾"]
Embroidery floss: black

Dimensional Diagram for Pass Case A

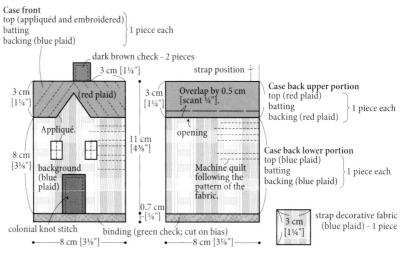

- When cutting appliqués, add 0.3 to 0.4 cm [⅛"] seam allowances. Do not add seam allowances to strap decorative fabric. Add 0.7 cm [¼"] seam allowances to all other pieces.
- For the binding, cut one bias strip 3.5 x 10 cm [1⅜" x 4"].

Dimensional Diagram for Pass Case B

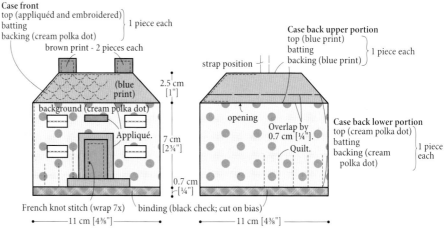

- When cutting appliqués, add 0.3 to 0.4 cm [⅛"] seam allowances. Do not add seam allowances to strap decorative fabric. Add 0.7 cm [¼"] seam allowances to all other pieces.
- For the binding, cut one bias strip 3.5 x 13 cm [1⅜" x 5⅛"].

6 Bind the bottom edge of the case with the green check bias binding strip. Make a loop at the end of the strap as shown in figure 7, sew in place, then bind with a strip of fabric to hide the knot.

Making Pass Case B

Although the designs are different, instructions are the same for both pass cases A and B. Please follow the steps for pass case A to make pass case B.

Figure 1: Appliquéing the case front

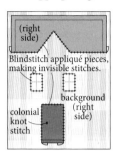

(right side)

Blindstitch appliqué pieces, making invisible stitches.

background (right side)

colonial knot stitch

Figure 2: Sewing the chimney

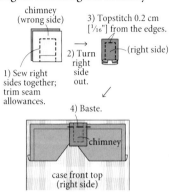

chimney (wrong side)

3) Topstitch 0.2 cm [¹⁄₁₆"] from the edges.

2) Turn right side out.

(right side)

1) Sew right sides together; trim seam allowances.

4) Baste.

chimney

case front top (right side)

Figure 3: Sewing the case front

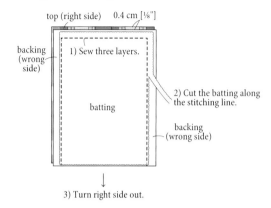

top (right side)   0.4 cm [⅛"]

backing (wrong side)

1) Sew three layers.

batting

2) Cut the batting along the stitching line.

backing (wrong side)

3) Turn right side out.

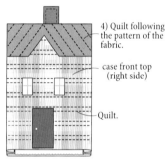

4) Quilt following the pattern of the fabric.

case front top (right side)

Quilt.

Figure 4: Sewing the case back upper portion

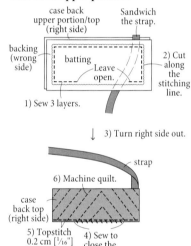

case back upper portion/top (right side)

Sandwich the strap.

backing (wrong side)

batting

Leave open.

2) Cut along the stitching line.

1) Sew 3 layers.

3) Turn right side out.

strap

6) Machine quilt.

case back top (right side)

5) Topstitch 0.2 cm [¹⁄₁₆"] from edge.

4) Sew to close the opening.

Figure 5: Sewing the case back lower portion

1) Sew 3 layers, leaving the bottom edge open; trim away the excess batting; turn right side out.

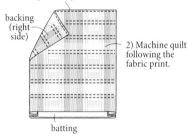

backing (right side)

2) Machine quilt following the fabric print.

batting

Figure 6: Joining the case front and back

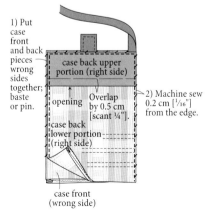

1) Put case front and back pieces wrong sides together; baste or pin.

case back upper portion (right side)

opening

Overlap by 0.5 cm [scant ¼"].

2) Machine sew 0.2 cm [¹⁄₁₆"] from the edge.

case back lower portion (right side)

case front (wrong side)

Figure 7: Sewing the strap

2) Fold 2 edges of decorative fabric square toward center to make a binding strip.

1 cm [⅜"]

(right side)

2 cm [¾"]

3) Machine sew.

4) Wrap binding strip around stitching and blindstitch in place.

Finished Pass Case A

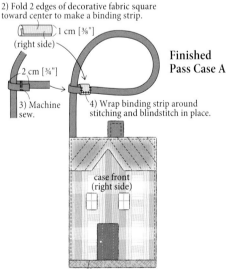

case front (right side)

1) Bind bottom edge with the 3.5 cm [1⅜"] wide bias strip.

Finished Pass Case B

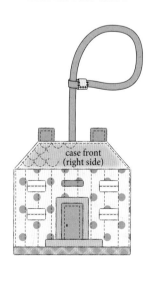

case front (right side)

Sewing Box shown on p. 42

Finished Measurements

- Side length: 8 cm [3⅛"]; width (w): 16 cm [6¼"]; depth (d): 10 cm [4"] (measurements do not include roof lid)
- The template/pattern can be found on side C of the pattern sheet inserts.

Materials Needed

Cottons

- Assorted fat quarters or scraps (approx. 30 pieces) (patchwork, appliqués, shingles A and B)
- Print A - 40 x 30 cm [16" x 12"] (box front, back, and sides)
- Print B - 40 x 15 cm [16" x 6"] (box bottom, patchwork)
- Print C - 50 x 15 cm [20" x 6"] (roof background)

- Check D - 3.5 x 16 cm [1⅜" x 6¼"] bias strip - 4 pieces (binding for roof side edges)
- Check E - 3.5 x 27 cm [1⅜" x 10⅝"] bias strip - 1 piece (binding for roof top edge)
- Print F - 20 x 10 cm [8" x 4"] (chimney top)
- Print G - 20 x 10 cm [8" x 4"] (chimney backing)
- Print H - 110 x 35 cm [44" x 14"] (box backing, inner pocket, roof backing, pincushion)
- Solid - 50 x 50 cm [20" x 20"] (box facing, roof facing)

Batting - 50 x 45 cm [20" x 18"]

Low-loft batting - 50 x 15 cm [20" x 6"] (roof)

Medium-weight interfacing - 45 x 40 cm [18" x 16"] (box backing, roof backing, inner pocket)

Heavyweight interfacing - 20 x 10 cm [8" x 4"] (pincushion)

Embroidery floss: brown, dark gray, gray

Template plastic (white) - 40 x 35 cm [16" x 14"]

Polyfill

Instructions

1 Referring to the dimensional diagrams below and on p. 91 and the full-size templates on side C of the pattern sheet inserts, sew together print A and B patches to make a pieced background for each section of the box top. Press patchwork seam allowances toward the upper edge. Stitch appliqués and embroideries onto each pieced background. (See figure 1 for the window appliqués.)

2 Sew together the box front, back, sides, and bottom to make one piece of fabric. Layer with batting and facing. Baste and quilt (figure 2). Draw finished (sewing) lines on the wrong side.

3 Make the inner pockets. Put them at the designated locations on the box backing. Sew along the bottom edges (figure 3).

4 Complete the box (figures 4 to 6).

5 Make shingles A and B (figure 7).

6 Make the roof (figure 8).

7 Complete the roof (figure 9).

8 Use the dimensions listed on p. 91 to make a pincushion. Blindstitch down to the inside of the roof (figure 10).

9 Make the chimney and blindstitch down to the roof (figure 11).

Dimensional Diagram (Continued on p. 91)

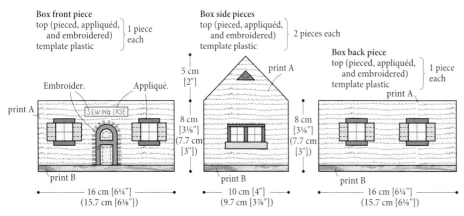

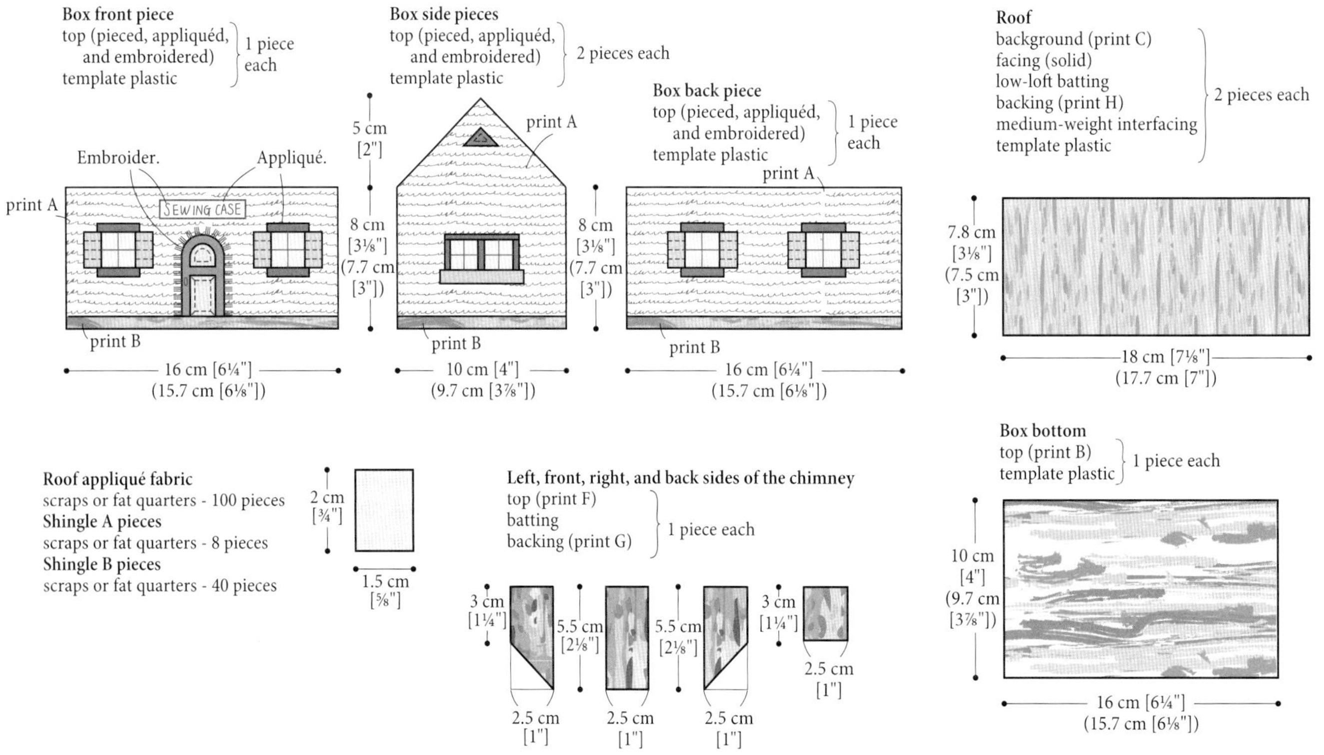

Box front piece
top (pieced, appliquéd, and embroidered) } 1 piece each
template plastic

Embroider. Appliqué.

print A

SEWING CASE

print B

16 cm [6¼"]
(15.7 cm [6⅛"])

Box side pieces
top (pieced, appliquéd, and embroidered) } 2 pieces each
template plastic

5 cm [2"]

print A

8 cm [3⅛"] (7.7 cm [3"])

print B

10 cm [4"]
(9.7 cm [3⅞"])

Box back piece
top (pieced, appliquéd, and embroidered) } 1 piece each
template plastic

print A

8 cm [3⅛"] (7.7 cm [3"])

print B

16 cm [6¼"]
(15.7 cm [6⅛"])

Roof
background (print C)
facing (solid)
low-loft batting
backing (print H)
medium-weight interfacing
template plastic } 2 pieces each

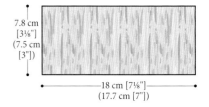

7.8 cm [3⅛"] (7.5 cm [3"])

18 cm [7⅛"]
(17.7 cm [7"])

Roof appliqué fabric
scraps or fat quarters - 100 pieces
Shingle A pieces
scraps or fat quarters - 8 pieces
Shingle B pieces
scraps or fat quarters - 40 pieces

2 cm [¾"]

1.5 cm [⅝"]

Left, front, right, and back sides of the chimney
top (print F)
batting
backing (print G) } 1 piece each

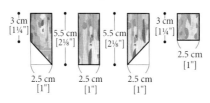

3 cm [1¼"]

5.5 cm [2⅛"]

5.5 cm [2⅛"]

3 cm [1¼"]

2.5 cm [1"]

2.5 cm [1"]

2.5 cm [1"]

2.5 cm [1"]

Box bottom
top (print B)
template plastic } 1 piece each

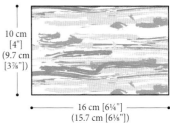

10 cm [4"]
(9.7 cm [3⅞"])

16 cm [6¼"]
(15.7 cm [6⅛"])

Dimensional Diagram (Continued from p. 90)

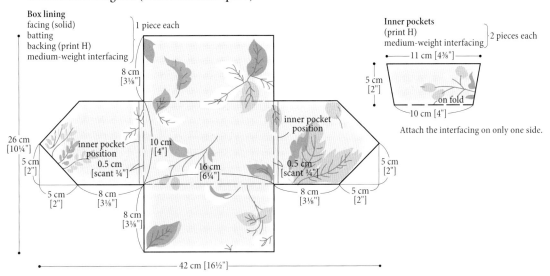

Box lining
facing (solid)
batting
backing (print H)
medium-weight interfacing
} 1 piece each

8 cm [3⅛"]

26 cm [10¼"]

5 cm [2"]

inner pocket position

inner pocket position

10 cm [4"]

0.5 cm [scant ¼"]

16 cm [6¼"]

0.5 cm [scant ¼"]

5 cm [2"]

5 cm [2"]

8 cm [3⅛"]

8 cm [3⅛"]

8 cm [3⅛"]

5 cm [2"]

42 cm [16½"]

Inner pockets
(print H)
medium-weight interfacing
} 2 pieces each

11 cm [4⅜"]

5 cm [2"]

on fold

10 cm [4"]

Attach the interfacing on only one side.

Pincushion
top (print H) - 1 piece
heavyweight interfacing
template plastic
} See figure 10.

4 cm [1½"]

4 cm [1½"]

13.7 cm [5⅜"]

template plastic

4 cm [1½"]

15 cm [5⅞"]

template plastic

20.7 cm [8⅛"]

Bias strip for roof side edges
check D - 4 pieces

3.5 cm [1⅜"]

16 cm [6¼"]

Bias strip for roof top edge
check E - 1 piece

3.5 cm [1⅜"]

27 cm [10⅝"]

- When cutting appliqués, add 0.3 cm [⅛"] seam allowances. Cut facing, batting, and low-loft batting with 3 cm [1¼"] seam allowances. Do not add seam allowances for heavyweight interfacing, medium-weight interfacing, template plastic, and bias strip for the roof. Cut all other pieces with 0.7 cm [¼"] seam allowances.
- Numbers in parentheses "( )" show template plastic dimensions; measure the dimensions of the sewing box after quilting to adjust the size of the template plastic as necessary.

Figure 1: Appliquéing windows

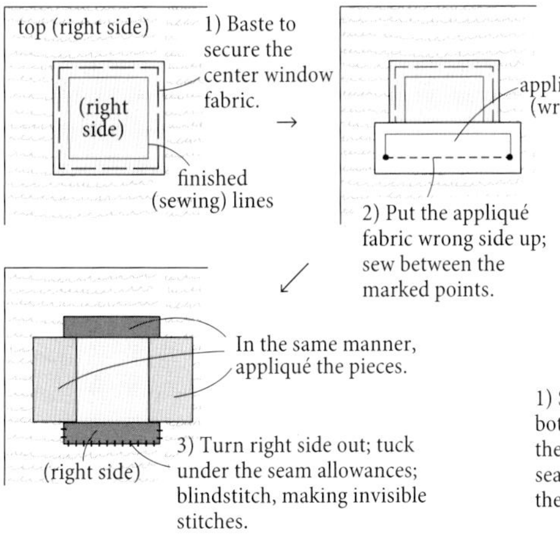

top (right side)

1) Baste to secure the center window fabric. →

(right side)

finished (sewing) lines

appliqué fabric (wrong side)

2) Put the appliqué fabric wrong side up; sew between the marked points.

In the same manner, appliqué the pieces.

(right side)

3) Turn right side out; tuck under the seam allowances; blindstitch, making invisible stitches.

Figure 2: Sewing top pieces together

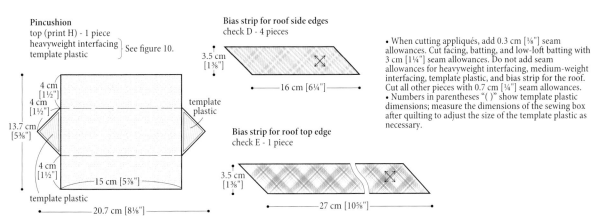

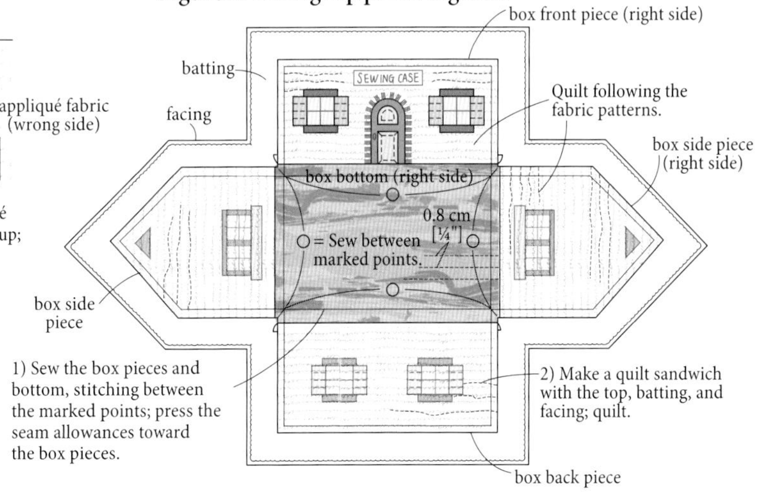

box front piece (right side)

batting

facing

SEWING CASE

Quilt following the fabric patterns.

box side piece (right side)

box bottom (right side)

0.8 cm [¼"]

○ = Sew between marked points.

box side piece

1) Sew the box pieces and bottom, stitching between the marked points; press the seam allowances toward the box pieces.

2) Make a quilt sandwich with the top, batting, and facing; quilt.

box back piece

91

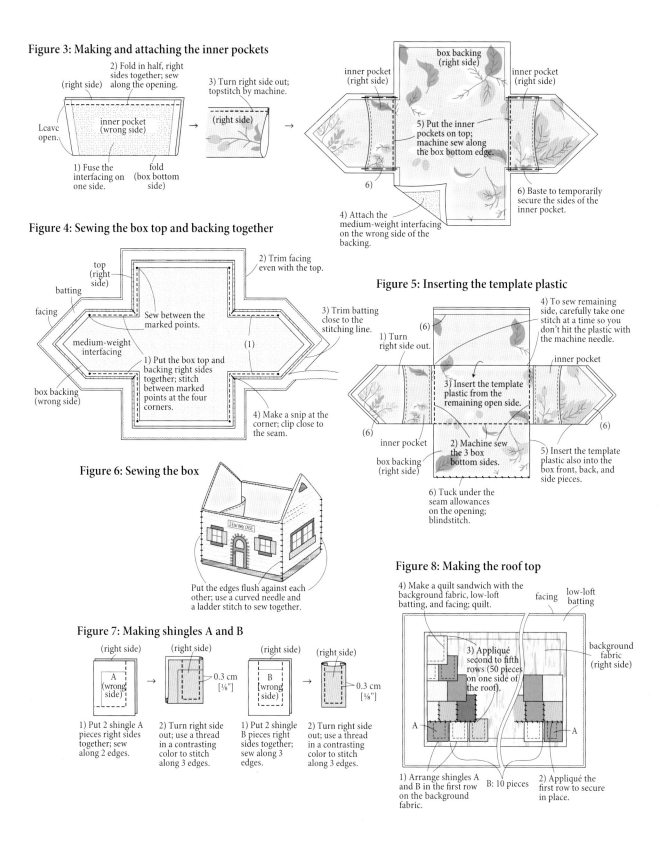

Figure 3: Making and attaching the inner pockets

(right side)

2) Fold in half, right sides together; sew along the opening.

3) Turn right side out; topstitch by machine.

Leave open.

inner pocket (wrong side)

(right side)

1) Fuse the interfacing on one side.

fold (box bottom side)

box backing (right side)

inner pocket (right side)

inner pocket (right side)

5) Put the inner pockets on top; machine sew along the box bottom edge.

6)

6) Baste to temporarily secure the sides of the inner pocket.

4) Attach the medium-weight interfacing on the wrong side of the backing.

Figure 4: Sewing the box top and backing together

top (right side)

batting

facing

medium-weight interfacing

box backing (wrong side)

2) Trim facing even with the top.

Sew between the marked points.

(1)

3) Trim batting close to the stitching line.

1) Put the box top and backing right sides together; stitch between marked points at the four corners.

4) Make a snip at the corner; clip close to the seam.

Figure 5: Inserting the template plastic

(6)

1) Turn right side out.

4) To sew remaining side, carefully take one stitch at a time so you don't hit the plastic with the machine needle.

inner pocket

3) Insert the template plastic from the remaining open side.

(6)

inner pocket

box backing (right side)

2) Machine sew the 3 box bottom sides.

5) Insert the template plastic also into the box front, back, and side pieces.

6) Tuck under the seam allowances on the opening; blindstitch.

Figure 6: Sewing the box

SEWING CASE

Put the edges flush against each other; use a curved needle and a ladder stitch to sew together.

Figure 7: Making shingles A and B

(right side)

A (wrong side)

1) Put 2 shingle A pieces right sides together; sew along 2 edges.

(right side)

0.3 cm [⅛"]

2) Turn right side out; use a thread in a contrasting color to stitch along 3 edges.

(right side)

B (wrong side)

1) Put 2 shingle B pieces right sides together; sew along 3 edges.

(right side)

0.3 cm [⅛"]

2) Turn right side out; use a thread in a contrasting color to stitch along 3 edges.

Figure 8: Making the roof top

4) Make a quilt sandwich with the background fabric, low-loft batting, and facing; quilt.

facing

low-loft batting

background fabric (right side)

3) Appliqué second to fifth rows (50 pieces on one side of the roof).

A

A

1) Arrange shingles A and B in the first row on the background fabric.

B: 10 pieces

2) Appliqué the first row to secure in place.

Figure 9: Sewing roof pieces together

1) Attach medium-weight interfacing to wrong side of the backing.

roof top (right side)
backing (right side)
medium-weight interfacing

2) Put top and backing right sides together; sew along the bottom edge, making sure that roof pieces A and B are not caught in stitches. Trim seam allowances even with top.

bias strip (wrong side)

6) Insert the template plastic; square up the edges.

facing
backing (right side)
Make 2 pieces.

5) Fold binding over seam allowances; blindstitch.

3) Turn right side out; sew 3.5 cm [1⅜"] wide bias binding strip to sides, right sides together. Trim seam allowances even with top.

0.7 cm [¼"]

4) Fold the bottom seam allowance toward the inside.

8) Put the 3.5 cm [1⅜"] wide bias strip on the roof top edge, right sides together. Sew between the marked points, carefully taking one stitch at a time so you don't hit the plastic with the machine needle.

0.7 cm [¼"]
1 cm [⅜"]
bias strip (wrong side)
3.5 cm [1⅜"]
top (right side)
backing (right side)

7) Put the two roof pieces wrong sides together.

9) Turn the bias strip right side out, fold it over the seam allowances, and blindstitch in place.

Figure 10: Making and attaching the pincushion

backing (wrong side)
(1)
(wrong side)

1) Fuse heavyweight interfacing to wrong side.

(2)
backing (right side)
(wrong side)

2) With right sides together, stitch between marked points.

3) With right sides together, sew all around, leaving open 7 cm [2¾"] to turn.

4) Turn right side out.

7 cm [2¾"]
(3)
top (right side)

5) Insert the triangle template plastic in both sides from the opening; stuff with polyfill and stitch opening closed.

6) Blindstitch pincushion to center of the inside of the roof using a curved needle.

roof inside
pincushion

6) Blindstitch the bottom edges of the chimney to the roof using a curved needle.

Figure 11: Making and attaching the chimney

1) Put the top and backing for each side of the chimney right sides together; sew between the marked points. (Be sure to leave the bottom edge open to turn right side out.)

(wrong side)
(right side)

2) Trim batting close to stitching line.

Leave open.

4) Machine quilt five vertical lines.

3) Turn right side out, and sew opening closed.

(right side)

Make the pieces for the other sides in the same manner.

5) Put the four chimney pieces wrong sides together; ladder stitch.

top (right side)

Finished Box

SEWING CASE

Glasses Case shown on p. 46

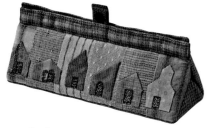

Finished Measurements
- Length (l): 6.3 cm [2½"]; opening width: 17 cm [6¾"]
- The template/pattern can be found on side D of the pattern sheet inserts.

Materials Needed
Cottons
- Assorted fat quarters or scraps (13 pieces) needed (for patchwork, appliqués)
- Polka dot - 10 x 5 cm [4" x 2"] (tabs)
- Check A - 20 x 20 cm [8" x 8"] (opening)
- Check B - 30 x 30 cm [12" x 12"] (gusset, backing)
Fusible fleece or single-sided fusible batting - 20 x 20 cm [8" x 8"]
Lightweight interfacing - 12 x 5 cm [5" x 2"]
Embroidery floss: gray, dark gray
Magnetic closure - 1 cm [⅜"] in diameter - 3 pairs
Plastic board - 20 x 20 cm [8" x 8"]

Instructions
1 Referring to the dimensional diagram on page 94 and the full-size template on side D of the pattern sheet inserts, piece patches together, then appliqué and embroider the case top. Put the case top and backing right sides together. Put the fusible batting on the wrong side of the backing, with the fusible side facing up. Sew along the sides. Trim off excess batting, turn right side out, and press to adhere the fusible batting (figure 1, steps 1 and 2).

2 Insert the plastic boards and machine sew to secure them (figure 1, steps 3 to 7).

3 Make the tabs (see figure 3 on p. 82). Sew the tabs to the case opening (figure 2).

4 Put the case top and one case opening (this will be the outer opening) right sides together. Sew along the opening between the marked points. Square up the edges and turn right side out. Put the magnetic closures at three locations on the wrong side of the remaining case opening (this will be the inner opening). Sew along both sides of the magnetic closures as shown, and blindstitch the inner opening (figure 3).

5 Make the gussets and position them at each end of the case body. Whipstitch to secure along two sides (figure 4).

Dimensional Diagram

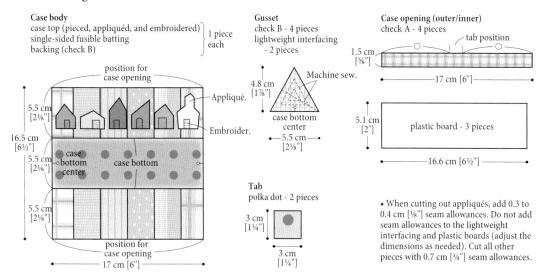

Case body
case top (pieced, appliquéd, and embroidered) ⎫
single-sided fusible batting ⎬ 1 piece each
backing (check B) ⎭

position for case opening

5.5 cm [2⅛"]

16.5 cm [6½"]

5.5 cm [2⅛"]

5.5 cm [2⅛"]

case bottom center

case bottom

Appliqué.

Embroider.

position for case opening

17 cm [6"]

Gusset
check B - 4 pieces
lightweight interfacing - 2 pieces

4.8 cm [1⅞"]

Machine sew.

case bottom center

5.5 cm [2⅛"]

Tab
polka dot - 2 pieces

3 cm [1¼"]

3 cm [1¼"]

Case opening (outer/inner)
check A - 4 pieces

tab position

1.5 cm [⅝"]

17 cm [6"]

5.1 cm [2"]

plastic board - 3 pieces

16.6 cm [6½"]

• When cutting out appliqués, add 0.3 to 0.4 cm [⅛"] seam allowances. Do not add seam allowances to the lightweight interfacing and plastic boards (adjust the dimensions as needed). Cut all other pieces with 0.7 cm [¼"] seam allowances.

Figure 1: Making the case

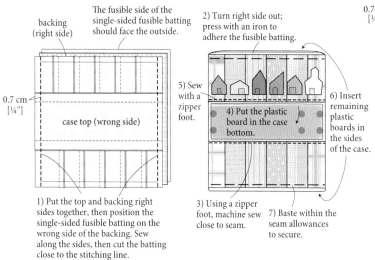

backing (right side)

The fusible side of the single-sided fusible batting should face the outside.

2) Turn right side out; press with an iron to adhere the fusible batting.

0.7 cm [¼"]

case top (wrong side)

5) Sew with a zipper foot.

4) Put the plastic board in the case bottom.

6) Insert remaining plastic boards in the sides of the case.

1) Put the top and backing right sides together, then position the single-sided fusible batting on the wrong side of the backing. Sew along the sides, then cut the batting close to the stitching line.

3) Using a zipper foot, machine sew close to seam.

7) Baste within the seam allowances to secure.

Figure 2: Making the case opening

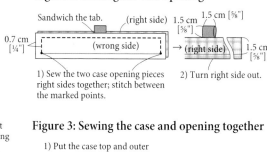

Sandwich the tab.

(right side)

1.5 cm [⅝"]

1.5 cm [⅝"]

0.7 cm [¼"]

(wrong side)

(right side)

1.5 cm [⅝"]

1) Sew the two case opening pieces right sides together; stitch between the marked points.

2) Turn right side out.

Figure 3: Sewing the case and opening together

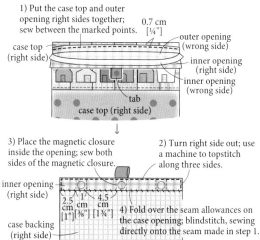

1) Put the case top and outer opening right sides together; sew between the marked points.

0.7 cm [¼"]

case top (right side)

outer opening (wrong side)

inner opening (right side)

inner opening (wrong side)

tab

case top (right side)

3) Place the magnetic closure inside the opening; sew both sides of the magnetic closure.

2) Turn right side out; use a machine to topstitch along three sides.

inner opening (right side)

2.5 cm [1"]

1 cm [⅜"]

4.5 cm [1¾"]

4) Fold over the seam allowances on the case opening; blindstitch, sewing directly onto the seam made in step 1.

case backing (right side)

Repeat to sew the opening to the other side.

Figure 4: Making and attaching the gusset

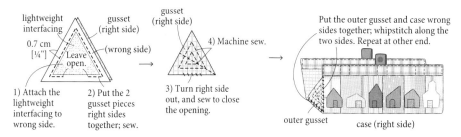

lightweight interfacing

0.7 cm [¼"]

Leave open.

gusset (right side)

(wrong side)

1) Attach the lightweight interfacing to wrong side.

2) Put the 2 gusset pieces right sides together; sew.

gusset (right side)

4) Machine sew.

3) Turn right side out, and sew to close the opening.

Put the outer gusset and case wrong sides together; whipstitch along the two sides. Repeat at other end.

outer gusset

case (right side)

94

Alsace Lorraine Wall Hanging shown on p. 48

Finished Measurements

- Length (l): 48 cm [18⅞"]; width (w): 48 cm [18⅞"]
- The template/pattern can be found on side B of the pattern sheet inserts.

Materials Needed

Cottons
- Assorted fat quarters or scraps (approx. 60 pieces) (appliqués)
- Print - 50 x 50 cm [20" x 20"] (background fabric)
- Check - 85 x 55 cm [34" x 22"] (backing, bias binding for seam allowances)

Batting - 55 x 55 cm [22" x 22"]
Embroidery floss: dark gray, gray, brown

Instructions

1 Referring to the dimensional diagram below and the full-size template on side B of the pattern sheet inserts, stitch appliqués and embroideries on the background fabric to make the quilt top. Blindstitch appliqué pieces to make individual house blocks, making invisible stitches. Start from the house at the farthest back (farthest away from you).

2 Make a quilt sandwich with the quilt top, batting, and backing. Baste and quilt (refer to the dimensional diagram).

3 Use a 2.5 cm [1"] wide bias strip to bind the quilt edges. Fold the seam allowance over and blindstitch down to the backing. (For a graphic finish to the wall hanging, the seam allowances and binding are pressed completely toward the backing.) See p. 68 for how to cut and join bias strips.

Dimensional Diagram

top (appliquéd and embroidered)
batting
backing (check)
} 1 piece each

Binding seam allowances

bias binding
backing
batting
top

- When cutting appliqués, add 0.3 to 0.4 cm [⅛"] seam allowances. Cut the background fabric with 1 cm [⅜"] seam allowances. Cut the batting and backing with 3 cm [1¼"] seam allowances.
- For bias binding to bind the quilt edges, from check cut 4 pieces 2.5 x 50 cm [1" x 19¾"].

background fabric

Quilt as desired following the fabric pattern.

Stitch in the ditch around the appliqué pieces and just outside the embroidered designs.

Embroider with an outline stitch around the window appliqués.

Appliqué.

48 cm [18⅞"]

48 cm [18⅞"]

Yoko Saito

Yoko Saito is a quilter, designer, and author of world renown. She studied both Japanese and western-style dressmaking, and became interested in learning to quilt after seeing antique quilts on a trip to America. Over the years, she found inspiration in Europe and Scandinavia, which is reflected in her unique use of colors and design. Her beautiful quilts and quilted works are exquisitely designed. Her intricate quilting and handwork techniques are based firmly in the basics of sewing. She teaches quilting at schools and through correspondence courses as well as on television shows. Her patterns are often published in magazines and she continues to release books each year. She is popular among quilters around the world and holds seminars and exhibitions overseas as her schedule allows.

Yoko Saito's Quilt School and Shop
Quilt Party Co., Ltd.
Active Ichikawa 2F
1-23-2, Ichikawa, Ichikawa-shi,
Chiba-Ken, Japan 272-0034

http://www.quilt.co.jp (Japanese)
http://global.rakuten.com/en/store/quiltparty/ (English)

Original Title	Saito Yoko no House Daisuki
Author	Yoko Saito
	©2019 Yoko Saito
First Edition	Originally published in Japan in 2017
Published by:	NHK Publishing, Inc.
	41-1 Udagawa-cho, Shibuya-ku,
	Tokyo, Japan 150-8081
	http://www.nhk-book.co.jp

Translation	©2019 Stitch Publications, LLC
English Translation Rights	arranged with Stitch Publications, LLC
	through Tuttle-Mori Agency, Inc.
Published by:	Stitch Publications, LLC, Seattle, WA, USA
	http://www.stitchpublications.com
Distributed exclusively by:	Martingale®
	19021 120th Avenue NE, Ste. 102
	Bothell, WA 98011, USA
	http://www.martingale-pub.com
Printed & Bound	KHL Printing, Singapore
ISBN	978-0-9863029-9-2
PCN	Library of Congress Control Number: 2019932447

Quilt Party Production Kazuko Yamada
Keiko Nakajima
Terumi Ishida
Akiko Koizumi

Staff

Book Design	Tomoko Nawata, L'espace
Photography	Akiko Arai
	Narumi Shimose
Stylist	Yoko Ikemizu
Instructional Text	Naoko Domeki, Chieko Sakuraoka
Illustrations	tinyeggs studio (Yumiko Oomori)
Proofreader	Hiroko Yamauchi
Editorial Assistant	Kyoko Masuzawa
Editor	Chiaki Takano (NHK Publishing, Inc.)

Photography Support AWABEES, TITLES, UTUWA

This English edition is published by arrangement with NHK Publishing, Inc., through Tuttle-Mori agency, Inc.